Men, Women, and the Power of Empathy

Men, Women, and the Power of Empathy

◆

You <u>Can</u> Really Connect with Him!

A.R. Maslow, Ph.D.

iUniverse, Inc.
New York Lincoln Shanghai

Men, Women, and the Power of Empathy
You <u>Can</u> Really Connect with Him!

iUniverse books may be ordered through booksellers or by contacting:

iUniverse
2021 Pine Lake Road, Suite 100
Lincoln, NE 68512
www.iuniverse.com
1-800-Authors (1-800-288-4677)

ISBN-13: 978-0-595-41492-5 (pbk)
ISBN-13: 978-0-595-85841-5 (ebk)
ISBN-10: 0-595-41492-3 (pbk)
ISBN-10: 0-595-85841-4 (ebk)

Printed in the United States of America

Contents

Acknowledgements

First, I would like to thank my friends and colleagues who have given me valuable support and helpful suggestions, including Dr. Randy Sights Baskerville, Jim and Genevieve Brigham, Dr. Russell Beale, Mark and Mary Maslow, Sid and Terry Burke, and Allen Steinhofel. I appreciate the assistance of Rebecca Barns, writer and editor, who helped me to write clearly, in good English. My thanks go to Barbara Lane, a talented and patient typist, who did an excellent job deciphering my handwriting and putting it in good form. And I want to thank Allen Steinhofel and Jim Bryan for generously coming to my rescue when I became stymied with computer problems.

I am very grateful to Rabbi David Cooper, an accomplished author, who encouraged me to continue the book project when I was not sure it was worth doing.

I want to give special recognition to Kevin Quirk, the writer and published author, who has been a major help in the entire book project. He has the extraordinary ability to grasp the essence of what I am trying to say, while helping me to say it better.

My wife, Carol, contributed to this book on several levels. She helped me with the writing, with her perspective as a woman and as a fellow therapist. What am I most grateful for is the relationship itself. It is the main place that, with Carol's help, I have learned, and am still learning, about defensiveness and empathy.

—A.R. Bob Maslow, Ph.D.

Introduction

After more than 30 years of professional experience working with couples, I've heard all the complaints women make about how men don't "get it" in their relationships: Why can't he just listen and try to understand my feelings and my experience? When we get into an argument, why does he always act like he's being attacked and tell me to stick to "the facts?" When I'm feeling upset about something, why does he always tell me I'm over-reacting? And when it's obvious that *he* is upset, why does he always insist that nothing is bothering him?

I've seen the long-term effects of women stewing in frustration over not being able to *really* connect with the man in their life. At the same time, I also have seen the pain in men who silently suffer from vulnerable feelings that they're usually not aware of and, even when they are, they fear the consequences of sharing them. I understand just how agonizing it can be to get stuck in this kind of relationship stalemate. Can anything help?

I'd like to offer an answer, and you may be surprised at how simple it sounds. The answer is *empathy*. I have found that empathy has the power to melt the coldest relationship logjams and ignite unexpected and exciting changes for couples willing to learn what it takes to practice it and commit to it. I also have found that while empathy is clearly more difficult for most men, they *can* get it—and their partners can have a lot to do with making it possible.

Before I begin explaining exactly how empathy works, what it can bring to your relationship, and what men *and* women need to know about breaking through his defenses that get in the way, let me explain how I came to such a strong belief in the power of empathy.

Several years ago a woman I was seeing in therapy was terribly upset, on the verge of terminating with me, because she thought that I had been dismissive of her in the way I ended our previous session. In the past, I would have tried to acknowledge and accept her upset feeling while also focusing on the issue of reality. Had I actually been dismissive? Was she distorting and/or over-reacting? Was she projecting the relationship she had with her parents onto me? I would try to be honest, but sometimes it was a hard balancing act. How sure could I be that I wasn't being defensive?

This time, I took a leap of faith and did something different. I just listened and gave my complete attention to simply understanding my client's experience, without any concern about the objective accuracy of her conclusions. Then something surprising happened. She was completely satisfied! She was no longer interested in looking further into whether I had or had not actually treated her badly in our previous session. It was clear that there was no residual harm to our relationship and, in fact, we seemed to be on even better footing than before.

I immediately began trying the same approach with other clients any time they expressed some dissatisfaction or complaint about something I had done or failed to do. I concentrated on just listening and encouraging them to express their feelings—to be empathic with no other agenda. Like that first woman, these clients also lost interest in their complaint because they could see that I was with them *in the present*, listening in a caring way to their feelings. In most cases, our relationship was strengthened. Of course I had always known that empathy is important in therapy. But something had shifted when I made it my primary focus when conflict was in the air.

Now I felt excited about the prospects of how this approach would work with couples. I began placing a much greater emphasis on helping couples to put aside concerns about objective reality, fairness, or self-protection so they could just listen to each other's feelings, experiences, and point of view. When couples were able to drop their defensive barriers enough to tap the power of empathy, a warm and loving connection suddenly emerged. Both partners felt more positive about their relationship. And while men, predictably, struggled more in trying to practice empathy, I found that with coaching they were frequently able to do it, much to the surprise and delight of their partners.

Ironically, despite what I had learned about the importance of empathy in working with couples, I ran into a similar problem in my own relationship. My wife Carol was upset about something I had done. She said that there was a certain way that I sometimes treated her that made her feel hurt and rejected. I felt very threatened by her words. I just couldn't accept the idea that I was doing this to her, and it certainly did not fit my image of myself as a caring, empathic partner. While I tried hard to just listen to Carol and understand her feelings, I was amazed by how difficult it was. Like many men I had seen in couples therapy, I found myself being defensive, arguing that she was misinterpreting my behavior. We were both frustrated, stuck in a painful impasse.

Finally, a light bulb went off. Everything I had been working on in therapy popped into my consciousness. I gulped, felt my anxiety, and let go of my defenses. I concentrated on just listening and tuning in to Carol's feelings, with no other agenda. The effect was immediate and powerful. Whereas before there had been an estrangement between us, now there was a melting, a feeling of warmth, a connection. Exchanges like this continued to happen from time to time, and the more they happened the easier it became for me to let go of my self-protective defenses. I felt relief in the understanding that I didn't have to defend past behavior. I got better at hearing Carol's feelings and treating them as valid. I also discovered another benefit of practicing empathy. I felt safer in exposing *my* feelings and counting on *her* to be empathic toward me. As a result, we became more relaxed with each other and closer than ever!

By then I was convinced of three things about relationships: One, dropping defensiveness and putting aside concerns about "right or wrong" so that we can listen empathically to our partners is a powerful catalyst for a successful relationship. Two, it is very difficult to do. Three, while women also may struggle with improving their ability to empathize with their partners, it really is more of a problem for men.

With that last point in mind, I realized that for couples to reap the benefits of empathy, they needed to gain a much better understanding of *why* men have such difficulty with it. Through my continued work with couples and empathy, I came to see how both partners usually lacked an understanding of the man's feelings, especially the vulnerable feelings behind his defensiveness. Without that understanding, and an environment in which he can begin to bring those feelings to light, the walls between them were likely to remain impenetrable. But when his unspoken vulnerable feelings such as hurt, shame, fear, or humiliation came out in the open, a powerful breakthrough in the couple's relationship was within reach.

That's why I wanted to write this book. In focusing on all the many benefits of empathy, I especially want to help you learn what goes on inside of men that makes it so hard for them to drop their defenses and really listen to their partner in an open, empathic way. What needs do they struggle to express? What conditioned roles keep them constricted and guarded?

As you will see in the chapters ahead, blaming your partner simply doesn't work. It's not good for him *or* for you. From all my years of working with couples and with men, I can assure you that behind that defensive mask he is suffering too. He may not show it, but the pain is there.

Also, it's vital that you understand all the reasons that mask stays in place. The truth is that you may be playing a part in how and why he decides that it is not okay or safe to disclose sensitive feelings and really listen to you. In my work, I have found that there is often a hidden collusion among men and women to deny or minimize his vulnerable feelings. So my goal is to help you and the man in your life work together to learn about feelings that men believe are unacceptable or a sign of weakness. You will then better understand how just giving men permission to feel those feelings has enormous power in the process of practicing empathy. Many forces have contributed to what threatens and shames him into building those walls of defensiveness, and you can work together to begin to tear those walls down.

As a couple, you also will learn:

- Why vulnerability is a sign of strength in a man, not a sign of weakness.

- How she can determine if she may not be communicating her *own* vulnerability and thus contributing to his defensiveness and lack of empathy.

- How he can drop his judgment and criticism and reveal his own feelings, and how she can talk to him so he can begin to risk opening up more.

- How he can break his tendency to rush in and "solve" the problem and instead pay attention to the more important feelings in the air.

- How he can begin to let go of his obsession with examining "the facts" to prove who is right and who is wrong, and how she can practice admitting to her role in the conflict.

- How to recognize the difference between false power and "real" power.

- What "clean" anger is and how to express it in a healthy way.

- How focusing on getting to know each other will work when negotiation and problem-solving will not.

- What a man can do to practice awareness of what he feels.

- How to view your relationship as a separate entity that needs to be cared for and nourished.

- Why it is critical for her to assure him that offering *him* empathy and emotional support is good for *her*, as well as for him.

- How the act of honestly acknowledging his deep need for his partner makes him feel far less alone.

- How it can help for both partners to recognize that they have "baggage" that they can work on and yet accept each other's emotional sensitivities that may never be overcome.

- How the warmth and connection that emerges through the power of empathy becomes a doorway for both partners into a deeper spiritual experience and union.

To help you learn these new tools, I have provided examples of many other couples stuck in typically frustrating patterns due to his lack of empathy and her inability to fully understand his vulnerability. You will see that when they unlocked the keys to empathy, profound changes ensued and their relationships became far more satisfying and harmonious. I will break down what these couples learned and how they practiced it, so that you can bring those skills into your relationship. When you do, you too will benefit from the powerful, lasting change that comes from understanding and practicing real empathy.

1

Why Practice Empathy?

It's the morning after the party, and the hot coffee contrasts sharply with the cold and icy glares Michelle is sending Charlie at the breakfast table. "You did it again," she finally snaps.

"What do you mean?" Charlie cuts in, bracing himself for a familiar argument.

"You ignored me at that party," she retorts.

"What the hell are you talking about? I spent time with you. I even danced with you," he insists.

"Yeah, one time," she counters, "like you were doing me a *favor*."

Feeling unjustly accused, Charlie searches for the facts that will prove his "case." He had joined Michelle when she was talking to their friends Jack and Evelyn, right? He had offered to get her something to drink, didn't he? "I even came over to you once when I saw you in that corner all by yourself," he adds.

Hearing this, Michelle pounds her mug down and bolts up from the table. They continue to argue over their different interpretations of exactly what did or did not happen at the party and what it really means. Of course, they get nowhere. Finally, Charlie grabs his car keys. "I'm gonna go play golf!" he growls. Minutes after he leaves, Michelle calls her best friend and laments to her about what happened. "That's awful. You must have felt really hurt," her friend responds after listening attentively. "Yeah, and ticked off too," Michelle adds. Though comforted by her friend's supportive ear,

Michelle still carries a lingering sense of feeling hurt, misunderstood, and uncared for by Charlie. Though she loves him, these are familiar feelings from the conflicts that have been repeated often in their twelve-year marriage.

At the golf course, Charlie stumbles through a series of bad shots as he mumbles to himself about the morning argument and how tired he is that these sharp disagreements keep happening. He cuts his round short after nine holes.

As he arrives home, Charlie gets his courage up and does something he has never done before. Approaching Michelle directly, he says, "I feel badly about what's happening between us. Let's start over." Surprised by this gesture, Michelle sits up straighter in her chair. "All right, fine," she says firmly, but without the bitterness of the morning. "This time, don't interrupt me and don't contradict me. Just listen." Charlie agrees to try. In doing so, he has just demonstrated his willingness to adopt the first important guideline that any man needs to follow in building lasting two-way intimacy (Note: I will be highlighting these guidelines throughout the book.):

- **When your partner complains about how you mistreated her, refrain from your usual tendency to defend yourself. Try instead to just listen to her feelings in the moment, to see things from her perspective.**

Feeling encouraged by Charlie's gesture, Michelle repeats much of what she had shared earlier in the day, stressing that she felt hurt and humiliated by his actions at the party. "I felt like I just don't matter to you," she says, fighting back the tears. She pauses, awaiting his response. She has noticed that so far he has refrained from turning into the "trial lawyer" rushing forward with his sharpest rebuttals. But would it last?

Charlie notices that he's still tempted to argue about the parts of Michelle's sharing that he does not agree with, but he knows where that always leads. And if they continue to argue like this, what might happen to their relationship? He doesn't want to think about that. Finally, he sighs and declares, "You're coming through loud and clear. I see how hurt you are and I can understand how you could feel that way."

- **As you listen, show her that you accept her feelings as valid, even though you may not agree with her.**

The effect for Charlie and Michelle is immediate and dramatic. They both relax and even begin to look each other in the eye. And, in softer and more respectful voices, they keep talking. While previously they had been at loggerheads, now there is warmth, a feeling of friendship. A door has been opened. They go on to discuss the incident in a way that recognizes not only Michelle's feelings but Charlie's needs and feelings as well.

What happened to make such a positive change possible? What went wrong in their morning argument about the party and what went right later? Some may conclude that Charlie and Michelle simply improved their communication, with Charlie the first to find a more effective way to communicate. After all, the experts say that good communication is the most critical ingredient for a positive relationship, right? But that word is too general to tell us what we really need to know about what worked so well for Charlie and what can open that door to a much closer and more loving connection in your own relationship. The word that best captures Charlie's new approach to Michelle is *empathy*.

We hear a lot these days about the trait or characteristic of empathy in discussions about relationships between a man and a woman, a parent and a child, and even an employer and an employee. But what does the word really mean? Empathy can probably be best understood as the ability to "feel into" the other person, to put yourself in their shoes and tune into their thoughts and feelings.

When you empathize with your partner, you gain a sense of what it is like to be her. This does not necessarily mean completely agreeing with or even sympathizing with what your partner is saying. Charlie certainly was not agreeing with everything Michelle was saying during their second attempt at discussing what happened at the party. Rather, it means that you understand how *she* feels and sees things at that moment, from *her* perspective.

Here are a few other ways to look at empathy:

- When you empathize, you don't simply tune into your partner's thoughts and feelings, you also *care* about them. They matter to you. You are not indifferent.

- When you are empathic you see your partner as a person in their own right. They are not a thing to be used to satisfy your wants and desires.

- When you see that your partner is unhappy or in physical or emotional pain, it arouses compassion in you.

- When you empathize with your partner, you validate them as a person. You are letting them know that they have the right to feel what they feel and be who they are.

- When you expect your partner to be empathic toward you, you feel empowered in the relationship because you know that he or she will be influenced by your feelings and needs. You also feel safe in exposing vulnerable feelings.

The central principle behind empathy is really very simple, and the overwhelming need for it in relationships crystal clear. If a woman reveals to her partner something personal and important to her—a complaint, a need, a longing—and her partner doesn't understand, or worse, dismisses her feeling, there is a serious break-down in the interaction and a critical loss for the couple. She feels not understood, not known, and not accepted by the most important person in her life. Each time this happens, the relationship is further weakened. The lack of empathy undermines trust and the willingness to be open, and the couple drifts further and further apart.

On the other hand, if her partner grasps her viewpoint or feeling, without evaluating or judging it, she feels validated, known, and accepted. This creates a sense of connection, strengthens trust in the relationship, and enhances each person's willingness to be open and close. The wellspring of warmth and love is tapped and begins to flow.

Can Men Really Be Empathic?

While the concept of empathy may be simple, actually practicing it is not at all easy for any of us. Most of us struggle with accessing empathy in some situations and encounters in everyday life. It's no secret, however, that practicing empathy is especially difficult and challenging for men. Many huge obstacles get in their way, and the task of removing or overcoming those obstacles takes a great deal of patience, awareness, and courage. It's not nearly enough to simply advise a man stuck in patterns of conflict with his partner to "just *listen* to her more. Women just want and need to be *heard*." Such typical and well-meaning advice misses the critical realm of *why* men struggle so much with empathy and what they, and their partners, must confront for men to become truly empathic partners.

Let's face it, most men enter into relationships poorly trained and poorly equipped to be empathic with their partner. Through social conditioning, men are taught to act tough, to be self-reliant, to keep the upper hand, and to never show their hurt, pain, or fear. They believe they must conceal how they need their partner because if she knew how much he needed her, she could exploit that knowledge and try to overpower or defeat him. They think they must always defend their actions and behavior so as to defend their turf and, hopefully, win the game or the battle. They grossly misjudge their woman's needs, and thereby resist tuning into her world, because they often see those needs as her way of trying to control him or make demands on him. Men also push into the background all their own softer, more vulnerable feelings because, to them, bringing out such feelings would be a sign of weakness. From dealing with everyone from the schoolyard bully to the corporate competitor, men have learned that it's dangerous to show any weakness at all.

Given that those are just a few of the many factors contributing to a man's inability to access or regularly practice empathy, is it any wonder that this void is so often named as a couple's Number One problem? In the chapters ahead, we will be exploring those challenges and obstacles that men face more fully, and I will offer many insights, examples, and guidelines on how men can begin to overcome them. I also will shed light on where women hit their own roadblocks on the road to building an empathic connection and how they can move through them. For now, it may be helpful to simply remember that women and men have had very different experiences in our society's changing gender roles of the last few decades.

As men can readily see, women generally have become more able to enter the domain of what used to be reserved only for men. Women have learned they can be more assertive and have at least begun to claim more authentic power in the boardroom, in the bedroom, and everywhere in between. But men, generally, still have not learned that they can be more emotionally open and vulnerable, and more sensitive to the feelings of others, without losing their essential masculinity. So, in the sea of change regarding the genders in our culture, men have remained behind, at times even adrift.

As a woman, bear this in mind as you relate to your partner who struggles with empathy. Understand that men really can learn this ability, and by reading this book with you he will be taking major steps toward becoming an empathic man. At the same time, recognize that *you* also have a critical role to play in the process of *his* uncovering his ability to become empathic. Throughout this book, I will be guiding you on how to understand and practice that role. In the sections titled "What the Woman Can Do," I will point out the mistakes that women unwittingly make in dealing with non-empathic men and provide concrete suggestions on the most effective ways to relate to him if you want to see that empathy you so deeply desire.

The Power of Empathy

Whether you are a woman or a man, you also will be learning what makes the effort totally worthwhile. You will be seeing and hearing what the power of empathy is all about. That power can be used to revive, change, or improve almost any kind of relationship, of course. But from my own life experience and more than thirty years of work as a couple's therapist, I have to say that nowhere is the power of empathy more dramatic and more valuable than in intimate relationships between men and women.

Why? Because empathy can be the key that cuts through all the trials and tribulations, all the challenges and obstacles that too often make our relationships seem almost impossible, despite our very best intentions. All of those obstacles disappear or recede into the background at the moment of an empathic connection. Empathy, then, is the track we can follow from which everything else begins to fall into place. It's one simple (but not easy) tool that makes the rest of the work so much easier.

As we've already seen with Charlie and Michelle, empathy builds trust and love, a sense of real togetherness. That togetherness provides a foundation for a more harmonious and caring approach in handling difficult matters around work, finances, children, sex, and a thousand and one other relationship issues. As Michelle illustrated in her response to Charlie, the receiver of empathy feels known and, more than that, recognizes that her partner cares enough to *want* to know her and not just stay wrapped up in his own world. The warm feelings that emerge through the power of empathy create a heart connection, which takes a couple beyond the complications of the mind, where matters of right and wrong tend to rule but no one really wins.

For a man, allowing his more vulnerable feelings to surface so that he can both become more empathic toward his partner and also receive more empathy from her, enables him to lower his guard. He can relax and see that he no longer has to drain his energy by putting up a front. For a woman, receiving empathy and being able to extend more empathy toward him melts the sense of despair she experiences in believing that the man in her life will never truly understand her. For both partners, the walls of isolation begin to crumble, walls behind which both she *and* he have suffered.

Of course, empathy seldom comes in a perfect form, and often it isn't particularly smooth. After all, we can't literally be inside another person. The power of empathy will always rise and fall in intensity and consistency. But once you have had a taste of empathy, you will never dream of going back to life without it.

Tapping the full power of empathy is not just a man's job. While empathy is much more often hidden beneath the surface for a man, it's important to understand that women also struggle with accessing empathy in their relationships. Even though women have had very different life experiences and cultural influences, they still will find that many of the examples and suggestions that follow will be equally applicable to them.

Let's begin with one of the most basic realities about empathy: To listen to your partner empathically often requires taking a risk.

If you have ever tried downhill skiing, you can probably relate to an experience of mine. When I first began to ski, I felt as if I had practically no control. My instructor kept telling me to lean downhill, explaining that doing so would put the weight on the balls of my feet and enable me to better control my skis. But instinctively, I wanted to do the opposite and lean back. Still, I understood the value of the instruction I was receiving and recognized that I had to do the opposite of what my instincts were telling me. By finally choosing to do what felt unnatural and scary—that is, by leaning downhill and forward—I wound up being more in control and was able to ski much better.

In some ways, my experience is similar to what is often required in an intimate relationship. When a conflict with your partner arises, you naturally feel a sense of danger, not unlike the beginning skier staring downhill from the top of the slope. When you feel that danger, your natural impulse is often to protect yourself, to avoid taking any risks. To take a risk by emotionally opening yourself to your partner seems foreign and even unwise. Yet taking a risk is exactly what's called for to access the power of empathy. So, just as I found in learning to ski, when you take a risk in your relationship you may discover that doing something that at first glance feels like the opposite of what is natural actually yields a greater payoff in the end.

Let's return to the example of Charlie and Michelle to see how Charlie was able to take a risk and listen to Michelle with empathy. Charlie felt threatened by Michelle's hurt and anger, and he felt accused of treating Michelle badly. Below the surface, he also feared that Michelle would take her reaction to what happened at the party and define him more sharply as an uncaring, unloving husband, and that eventually she might even leave him! Needless to say, Charlie felt a strong sense of danger in the midst of this conflict. Much of this danger was not new to him. For years he had been wrestling with his insecurities with Michelle. Early in their marriage he even used to worry whether she had really wanted to marry him, even after she had assured him that she most certainly did. On top of all this, while Charlie may have actually felt badly about causing Michelle pain long before he admitted that to her, this was a threat to the "nice guy" image he liked to hold of himself.

Yet even as this danger led Charlie initially to protect himself against Michelle, he eventually did let go of defending himself. He took that risk. He still felt fear, but he leaned down that hill and went racing toward a posture of empathic listening. What enabled him to go forward? Well, part of the motivation came from recognizing that the old ways just didn't work. Many times with Michelle in the past, Charlie had defended himself against whatever he felt accused of. He kept his guard up. And each time, the conflict only escalated and the distance between them grew. Now, the pressure of failing again was even scarier because he believed the fate of the relationship itself was in jeopardy. The danger had intensified, so the risk of not changing at all became greater than the risk of trying something new.

- **Take the risk to be empathic even if it feels unnatural or the opposite of what may make sense to you. It's a far greater risk to continue the ways that don't work.**

Something else was happening to Charlie as he found the courage to choose empathy. He could hear a whisper inside himself telling him that he was hiding something, that maybe he really had acted inappropriately at that party. It's that whisper we hear when we don't want to admit something but we know it's there, a whisper that's hard to ignore forever. Any man seeking greater intimacy should make a great effort not to ignore it.

- **If you suspect you are hiding the truth about how you contributed to the conflict, listen to that whisper. It takes guts to be honest with yourself.**

Now let's look more closely at what Charlie gained by taking the risk and tapping the power of empathy. The close connection he experienced with Michelle after listening empathically to her enabled him to feel more secure in the relationship. Rather than hearing her criticism that stirred up his insecurities, he experienced her warmth, her appreciation, and her willingness to reach out to him. He sensed that he was acceptable to Michelle even though he was flawed, and that security made it easier for Charlie to look at himself more closely. As their discussion continued that day, he was emboldened to take the next step and get in touch with feelings previously kept out of his conscious awareness. For example, he was able to see, and to acknowledge to Michelle, that before the party he had recently been feeling criticized in general by her and that he felt rejected sexually. So when he was keeping his distance from her and perhaps gravitating toward other women a bit more at that party, he was trying to get back at her and boost his ego.

In expressing these vulnerable feelings, Charlie was now the one in need of understanding and acceptance from Michelle. She responded in the same spirit of having received empathy from Charlie by just listening to his feelings as *his feelings*, without launching into a debate about the recent past. He got his turn to share honestly about what was happening for him, and the response was very positive. This is an important realization for any man to make when he is tempted to instantly defend himself, even before the full heat of the battle.

You will recall that when Charlie and Michelle launched their initial verbal assaults at the breakfast table, Charlie went off by himself to play golf. That gave him time to cool down and reflect a little. When he came back later, he was much more ready to take that risk to express empathy to Michelle. Then, later that same day, Charlie had his chance to share his feelings. When he did, he discovered as an added bonus that Michelle was even able to admit that she felt a bit intimidated by the people she didn't know at the party and, therefore, may have been holding herself back from more social contact. So it wasn't just a matter of him "ignoring" her. The power of empathy had now come full circle, and the benefits continued to expand for both of them. And it all began because Charlie was able to allow himself to feel his fear while listening to Michelle without defending himself.

Interactions like this one between Charlie and Michelle do not always go smoothly, of course. Couples trying to practice empathy, especially if it has mostly been hidden for him, usually hit many stops and starts along the way. But each time they are able to return to the essence of empathy, the road gets smoother. They have crossed a turning point.

Becoming a Different Person

Let's look at how this turning point opened the door to greater closeness for another couple. Gloria and Michael, a couple that I had been seeing in therapy, had no trouble identifying the source of their most intense conflicts. Michael was several years older than Gloria, and both would agree that he sometimes assumed a wiser, more superior posture toward her. In Gloria's view, Michael's acting superior took the form of consistently discounting and devaluing her feelings and her ideas. "Yes, Mister Know It All," she often cracked to him.

Michael would try to let these remarks slide off his back. Anyway, in his view Gloria was constantly leaning on him and expected him to have all the answers, which he was quick to point out to her. That would lead to both sides feeling accused and blamed. Recently in couple's therapy, they had begun to address these issues and at least had succeeded in listening to each other's perspective for a moment or two before launching into old disagreements. They had taken a step forward but had not yet solved the problem in day-to-day life together.

The conflict came to a head the day Gloria approached Michael feeling eager to share what she had just learned about potential new options for their financial investments. She told Michael that she was concerned about a recent slide in the stock market and the overall direction of the economy. Feeling confident, she informed him that she had just read some material that pointed to a wiser course. Michael wasn't buying any of it. "The market goes up and the market goes down. You're just being a pessimist," he replied in a condescending tone that was all too familiar to Gloria.

Suddenly, Gloria exploded. "If Harry had shared this information with you, you'd listen to him!" she snapped. "Anybody but me, you'd take them more seriously. You treat me like I'm stupid, Michael, and I'm *sick* of it!" Feeling stung, Michael snapped back, "Yeah, but when problems come up, you always make *me* the one who has to know what to do!"

For the next hour, they stewed in their tension and pain. During that time Michael took a hard look at himself. He kept hearing the echoes of what Gloria had said about him a few moments earlier, and was struck by how often he had heard it from her before. He couldn't see what she was talking about, yet there was a small voice telling him that there was something to it. When he finally broke the silence between them, his condescending tone was gone. "It's hard for me to admit that there is some truth to what you're saying, but there is," he said softly. "Now tell me again what you read and what you'd like us to consider doing differently with our investments."

This time, Michael focused on really listening to Gloria as if she knew something. He found himself relating to her differently, as more of an adult—an equal. It was as if he was seeing a different person. Maybe she could actually teach him something and he could benefit from her contribution. He suddenly felt more appreciative of her, with a growing respect and even a growing love. He had always loved her, of course, but now that love had a different quality to it. As he recognized the difference, he felt a sense of sadness over the limits to how he had been loving her in the past. Still, he tried not to beat himself up over this, remembering something I had discussed with him in couple's therapy: What really matters is how you treat your partner *now*, not what you did before. And remember that you are changed too. You are not the same person.

Gloria and Michael pored over the details of the new investment possibilities together over the table, working as a team. They paused for a moment to share a hug. A few minutes later Gloria put down the investment brochures, looked at Michael, and said, "It wasn't always you devaluing me. I know I put you on a pedestal myself." Gloria and Michael had just discovered that when you risk being less defensive and more honest, it makes it easier for your partner to do the same.

They had reached their turning point. Where just minutes earlier there had been coldness and distance between them, now there was warmth, a real melting. It wasn't that everything in their relationship had been resolved. Rather, they had reached a new place, and from there they were able to look at the relationship and begin to restructure how they could relate to each other in a healthy and positive way. It was the simple shift of Michael listening without defending that opened the door. From all my work with couples, I know that what may appear as a small and simple shift can make the huge difference between a relationship that keeps breaking down and one that is fully repaired and strengthened.

Putting Aside "Objective Reality"

As we did with Charlie, let's try to understand more fully what made the shift difficult for Michael in the first place. Then we will explore what enabled him to move forward and tap the power of empathy during his argument with Gloria over financial investments. Remember, Michael felt accused of hurting his wife by discounting her feelings and opinions. He, of course, did not want to believe that he had harmed her, nor did he want to see himself as someone who needed to devalue his wife and thereby maintain a superior attitude. So some degree of feeling threatened and defensive was certainly understandable, but the degree of Michael's reaction during their flare-up went way beyond that.

Michael's over-reaction was based on two common errors that men make with their partners. First, he believed that Gloria's complaints meant that she regarded him as primarily to blame for all their marital difficulties, meaning that he was totally unacceptable to her. Earlier, when Gloria would make those little digs about being "Mister Know It All," he was sometimes able to just let it go. But when she exploded in anger the day they discussed their investments, it woke him up. He took her outburst as an attempt by "Judge Gloria" to condemn him as the perpetrator of an unforgivable crime! She seemed totally fed up with their relationship, and that left him feeling extremely threatened. So he believed he had to do or say something to make her wrong and somehow win the argument in order to rescue himself and save the relationship.

In actuality, even when Gloria said she felt like Michael was treating her like a child and she was sick of it, she was just expressing her anger *in the moment*. She was trying to communicate that there was something wrong with what was happening during the argument. All the while, she continued to regard their relationship and its basic value to her as a solid given. For her, the foundation of their relationship was simply not at question. Michael missed that.

Michael's second error was that, like Charlie, he chose a method of dealing with the conflict that just doesn't work. He launched his defense by resorting to a stream of "objective reality," falsely assuming that proving himself right was the only way to get through to Gloria and end the disagreement. So as his argument with Gloria intensified that day, he went on to lecture her more about the ups and downs of the stock market and the economy and how well he understood it all. Had the argument continued even further, he would have went on to list all the successful investments he had made in his life and dredged up any supporting evidence he could point to where Gloria had made even the slightest financial mistake of her own in the past. He would have used anything to keep building his case, while all along the way deepening the divide between them.

How did Michael change his approach and try practicing empathy? Well, just being able to talk about his hot-button issues in couple's therapy earlier may have helped him feel safer in the relationship so he could take a risk that day. Or he may have simply over-ridden his fear because he felt more ready to face himself and his own vulnerability. Perhaps it was a combination of both.

Once he took the plunge, Michael made some startling discoveries. It turned out that Gloria was not totally rejecting him, despite the intensity of her explosion. Anyway, he learned that what really mattered to Gloria was not how he had treated her in the past but his new willingness to be with her *in the present*, even when she was expressing harsh feelings. In fully listening to her, he was showing her the respect and caring she felt had been missing. That was far more convincing to her than any verbal defense built on objective reality. What a relief for Michael, and for any man, to see that! Michael also learned that Gloria really just wanted him to treat her feelings and opinions about the investments as valid. It was not critical to Gloria that he agree with her at all. Realizing this, Michael could let go of arguing over who was right and who was wrong and tune into Gloria's perspective more openly.

In their new shared warmth and mutual respect, Michael made a further discovery. After Gloria felt really heard and valued, she was able to let go of her one-sided view of being the victim in their conflicts and admit that she had been putting Michael on a pedestal and thus contributing to the problem. She felt safe enough to acknowledge her "stuff."

Now let's flash forward to the next scene at their table that day. It turns out that Michael was able to express more of *his* feelings. He told Gloria that he realized he had been afraid that if he treated her as an equal, she would not need him anymore and would leave him. Upon hearing this, Gloria got up from her chair, came over, and gave Michael a big hug. So, as it often happens when the power of empathy is put into motion in our relationships, what starts out as one person wanting desperately to be heard ends up with both partners opening up to each other and becoming much closer.

What the Woman Can Do:

What about Gloria's part in the dramatic move toward practicing empathy that she and Michael made? As you may remember, I mentioned earlier in the chapter that women have a critical role in making it less threatening for a man to become empathic. So let's look at how Gloria did in relating to Michael. First, once he had taken the big step to begin listening to her without defending himself, she came forward and admitted that it wasn't always Michael at fault in their conflicts. She knew she had contributed to the ongoing problem.

- **Whenever you can, share with him the part you know you have been playing in the conflict. Let him know that you can understand how he might have been feeling hurt or threatened by you.**

Doing this will almost always have a very positive effect. Of course, I realize that in the heat of an argument it's very difficult to stop and say something like, "Maybe I'm especially sensitive in this area," or "I'm not saying that I'm a hundred percent right and you're a hundred percent wrong." But minutes or even hours after your flare-up, it's not too late to share your own accountability. When you do, you will greatly enhance the chances of your partner cooling down and stepping toward empathy much sooner.

Also, be aware if you sometimes try to zing your partner during an argument by calling him names like "selfish" or "immature." Obviously, such remarks only fuel the flames of the conflict. He will just get even more angry and defensive, and your chances of getting an empathic response from him sink even lower.

- **Absolutely avoid impugning your partner's character by using such labels as "selfish" or "immature," and also refrain from characterizing his behavior as "insensitive" or "uncaring." Stick to sharing your *feelings*.**

Usually, what is behind the put-down is anger. If you find that is true for you, try telling him you're angry while you try to access your hurt feelings underneath. But we're all human. If you do wind up just venting your anger at him, and it comes out all wrong, simply recognize that he will become more defensive. Back off for a few moments and try again.

- **Ask yourself if you are just trying to punish him, trying to make him feel guilty or small, instead of simply expressing your anger. Come back later when your anger has subsided or is less intense and try to show your underlying vulnerable feelings, like hurt or fear.**

At some point in your interaction, make a softening statement such as, "I know you didn't do what you did maliciously or to try to hurt me, but that's how I felt." Returning to the example of Charlie and Michelle, consider how Michelle might have softened her statements to Charlie about his behavior at the party. She might have said something like, "I know that you like feeling free and meeting new people." Then, when she went on to share her hurt about how she felt ignored, she might have had a better chance of Charlie listening to her because he wouldn't have experienced her reaction as a major assault to defend against.

In Gloria's situation, she might have employed a more effective strategy as soon as Michael started running through all "the facts" about the stock market and the economy. The natural tendency for a woman getting presented with the facts that support his case is to counter with what she believes are the tougher facts that will tilt the case in *her* favor. Instead, the two sides just keep swapping charges and counter-charges, all in the name of who has "the truth" behind them. So any woman tempted to get caught up in the battle of facts will benefit by taking this approach:

- **When he steers the argument toward the facts, let him know that you would like to let go of the facts for now and just deal with each person's feelings. Assure him that you will be willing to explore the issue more completely later.**

If Gloria had reminded Michael that facts are not everything, it might have helped him to relax, even if for a moment, and more easily find his way toward empathy sooner. As a woman, you have many other ways to help. For one, make sure that any time your partner is able to practice a degree of empathy and just listen to you that you avoid any temptation to use the opening as an invitation to rush in with all your other grievances about him. You certainly can't expect to get him to listen to every one of them all at once, anyway, and you would be missing out on a golden opportunity. During the argument or in its aftermath, if you can legitimately acknowledge any way that you have seen your partner trying to do better with his pattern of behavior that most hurts you, share that with him.

- **Whenever he is able to listen to your feelings, acknowledge him and express your appreciation. Positive reinforcement works.**

You can make other positive responses during a tense situation. Suppose you sense that when your partner did something that hurt you, he was merely acting out of anger toward you. In that situation, it can be effective to say, "Maybe you were feeling annoyed with me." Also, if an argument ends in a painful stalemate, try to avoid always rushing to your women friends to voice your despair about not being close to your partner and your belief that he won't ever change. It's great to have friends who understand and support you, of course, and it can be beneficial to turn to them at times. But ultimately, if you rely *only* on your friends for open sharing and support, you will just build a wall between you and your partner.

Anyway, the truth is that he is suffering, too. This is very important for you to understand. When he's always trying to defend his way out of an argument, you may see him as the Top Dog and believe that since he's keeping the upper hand he can't be feeling any pain. That's a distortion of reality. As we'll explore in later chapters, men often feel just as threatened and just as hurt by relationship conflicts as you do, though they seldom show it directly. So if you really want to create change, you need to stay in the same arena with him and figure it out together.

It also helps to be patient with a man trying to learn to practice empathy. Understand that men are more oriented toward action than in connecting through words. So he naturally interprets your complaints as not just a criticism but a demand that he do something to change his behavior, and that changing his behavior is the only thing you will accept. Help him see that your goal is more for him to listen in a way that recognizes that your feelings are legitimate, so you can feel cared for and connected. After that, it will be easier to talk about possible behavior changes, if and when that is even really necessary.

Also, it's not reasonable to expect either for you *or* him to be empathic all the time. It's not even a good idea for him to *try* to be empathic in every challenging situation. If he did, he would probably be blocking his own needs, feelings, and spontaneity. Sometimes he may be too tired or too preoccupied to listen empathically. If he forced himself to listen at such moments, his attempts would be half-hearted and leave you disappointed, or he might feel that he was being overly self-sacrificing and therefore become resentful. If he indicates in some way that he would like to hear you but can't right now, give him room. And sometimes his needs may be so compelling that he needs you to listen to him before he can really hear you. Be flexible.

Men also need to be flexible and patient with themselves and with their partner. Practicing empathy yields great power, but it's often not easy to tap into it. To take the risk and choose empathy means risking *yourself*, because you are making yourself more open and vulnerable with your partner. You may get hurt or sometimes shaken up along the way, but what you get in return is a vital sense of yourself growing stronger as a person and the incomparable reward of real intimacy.

So now that you've gotten a glimpse as to the true power of empathy in our relationships, you're ready to go further in our exploration. In the following chapters, you'll learn much more about what gets in the way of empathy and what men *and* women can do about it. And you'll see more fully all the rich rewards to be reaped when we really practice it.

Summary Guidelines

For the Man:

1. When your partner complains about how you mistreated her, refrain from your usual tendency to defend yourself. Try instead to just listen to her feelings in the moment, to see things from her perspective.

2. If you know you can't sincerely listen to her because you're having overwhelming feelings of your own, take time out and come back later. Remember, you will get your turn to share your feelings with her and that it's good to stake your right to do it.

3. As you listen, see if you are able to say something like, "I can see how that could have hurt you." This shows her that you accept her *feelings* as valid, even though you may not agree with her "facts" or conclusions.

4. Recognize that being empathic seems risky and may feel unnatural. Understand that it's a far greater risk to continue the ways that don't work.

5. If you hear a whisper that says you are hiding a truth about yourself and how you have contributed to the conflict, listen to it. It's an opportunity to be honest with yourself and with your partner.

6. If you get caught in your defensiveness the first time, come back later when you are calmer and try again.

For the Woman:

1. Avoid impugning your partner's character by using such labels as "selfish" or "immature," and refrain from characterizing his

behavior as "insensitive" or "uncaring." Stick to sharing your feelings.

2. Ask yourself if you are just trying to express your feelings or if you are trying to punish him and make him feel bad. If he feels punished he is less likely to be open and available to you. If you suspect that you have made that mistake, or that he took it that way, try to show your underlying vulnerable feelings like hurt or fear.

3. When he steers the argument toward the "facts" let him know that you would like him to let go of the facts for now and just deal with each person's feelings. Assure him that you will be willing to explore the issue more concretely again later.

4. After you have expressed your feelings, share with him the part you know you have been playing in the conflict. Let him know that you can understand how he might have been feeling hurt or threatened by you.

5. Whenever he is able to listen to your feelings, acknowledge him and express your appreciation. Positive reinforcement works.

2

Learn How Vulnerability Makes You Stronger

Putting the power of empathy into practice in our relationships challenges us to be comfortable with our feelings. For men, that's a real problem. How can we be comfortable with something we've been taught to avoid for most of our lives? How do we embrace that which we believe we must shun at all costs? How can we even begin to re-program a system that for many of us was entrenched before the age of the computer?

Some background may help. We men grow up with all kinds of messages telling us what it means to be a man. Some of these messages are adaptive and valuable, but others are distorted and destructive. The emphasis on power and toughness helps us to stand up for ourselves, to not allow ourselves to be taken advantage of or be pushed around. In sports or in dealing with corporate or political infighting, the goal is to be brave, to be strong, and to win. Also, what we learn about the importance of toughness and courage can be beneficial when we have to face the inevitable hardships and blows of life. While the values in themselves are important and serve us well in many ways, the truth is that we also pay a huge price in how we are taught these values and in our efforts to live up to them.

What we are told over and over again is that certain feelings are not permissible, that they are not manly. Feelings like hurt, shame, inadequacy, and even sadness and fear are the kinds of emotions that *women* feel and express. They're not for men. We men are not supposed to experience such feelings, or certainly not to any major degree. When they begin to bubble up, we must put a lid on them. Get hold of ourselves. Suck it up. And even if we do feel any vulnerable feelings, we tell ourselves that we can't show that to others. That would mean we are not in control, not on top of the situation, not a man. Sharing vulnerable feelings could mean being judged, taken advantage of, or defeated. Above all, we men believe we must avoid the terrible humiliation of appearing weak and being branded "not a man."

As a result, men believe that the act of suppressing feelings, especially vulnerable feelings, is absolutely necessary to survive and adapt. "I have to deal with this on my own," we tell ourselves. "I'll just ride it out until it goes away. No one else needs to know about it." And in our relationship we tell ourselves that showing vulnerable feelings might make her think less of us. She may think we're not a man—we're a wimp.

Men, these beliefs are totally misguided. They are destructive to us as individuals and they cause serious problems in our relationships with the women in our lives. The point is that feeling hurt, feeling inadequate, feeling ashamed, feeling threatened—these are human feelings that we all experience at times, especially in our intimate relationship. When we experience her disapproval, criticism, or rejection, we are going to feel some kind of emotional pain. There's no denying it. And when we do deny it, if we try to talk ourselves out of those feelings, we are being false to ourselves. That falseness weakens us. And if we are self-critical, thinking we are being unmanly, we further weaken ourselves.

What about men who are hyper-sensitive, who feel criticized or rejected way beyond the reality of how their partner is really feeling and behaving? Most of us have had early family experiences that have made us overly sensitive in certain areas. What works is to openly admit the truth of your feelings, and for both you and your partner to recognize that this is an area where you are sensitive and your button gets easily pushed.

Yes, there are times when we need toughness, and there is a certain strength that comes from that. Yet there is another, deeper strength that can only come from being real, *accepting who you are*, including your vulnerability.

• **Admit that your partner can hurt you by her actions and words. Claim your right to human vulnerable feelings, and be proud that your are willing to open yourself to an intimate relationship.**

Honestly facing your vulnerable feelings and sharing them with those closest to you in your life is an act of *strength*. It is a healthy and critical component not only of a great relationship but also a harmonious and satisfying life. Rather than a weak trait, it is a strong and vital one that can serve you in many powerful ways. By taking emotional risks and putting yourself out there, you improve and even transform your relationships. In the process, you also boost your self-esteem and enhance your own personal growth.

As this chapter unfolds, we will explore just how and why that is true. We also will look at how women often collude in the process of men not showing their vulnerability, even if they don't intend to, and what women can do to change those tendencies and instead support and encourage men in striving toward vulnerability.

Hidden vs. Open Vulnerability

To help understand how this issue operates in the lives of men, it helps to break down vulnerability into its two different forms. The first form is *hidden vulnerability*. This is the kind that is internal, or unexpressed. A feeling may begin to stir inside, but you criticize yourself for having it and so hide or suppress it. As that feeling stewing in you escalates, you still just want to make it go away and so try to stuff it down further and further. You deny having it to yourself and deny its existence or its importance to your partner.

Here's an illustration of how hidden vulnerability sabotages a relationship. Jason has just made plans for Saturday for him and Cindy, and he is very excited about them. He was able to make reservations at that restaurant that usually books up well before the weekend, and he bought the last tickets to the play everyone at work has been talking about. Only problem is, when he tells Cindy about "their" plans, he learns that she already had made a commitment to spend the late afternoon and evening with a friend visiting from out of town. Jason realizes right away that Cindy had mentioned something about this, but he had forgotten. Now, he feels that his balloon has been punctured.

While Cindy recognizes and acknowledges that Jason may have had a positive intention, she also knows that this kind of "forgetting" and discounting her plans is part of a familiar pattern. She complains to him for ignoring her needs, especially since she had made it a point to fill him in about her friend coming. She also explains that it felt like he was being inconsiderate by not at least asking her if his plans for Saturday sounded good to her before he made them.

Internally, Jason is feeling sad that his plans won't come off and hurt by Cindy's complaints about him. Also, he feels at least a tinge of guilt and shame for the part of her complaint that may be justified. Maybe he *was* being inconsiderate when he didn't check in with her before making those plans. More important, he feels threatened, afraid that Cindy's criticisms of him will continue to intensify and cause more turmoil and conflict in their relationship. These are all natural feelings. But rather than stop and acknowledge any of these vulnerable feelings to himself or to Cindy, Jason stuffs them inside and pretends they really don't exist or don't matter. He is stuck in hidden vulnerability.

So what does he do? He attacks and defends. He makes excuses for forgetting that Cindy had informed him that she had made other plans. "You didn't really say that you made plans with your friend, only that you were considering it," he insists. "I try to do something good for us and you just criticize me." He also makes her wrong for unfairly criticizing him for those past incidents when she thought his behavior was inconsiderate. As their argument continues, he goes on denying his real feelings that have surfaced and that continue to stir in him.

Now suppose Jason had reacted very differently. Imagine that at some point during the argument he had said to Cindy, "You're right. Maybe I did forget that you cleared it with me to go out with your friend. Anyway, I was wrong for not asking you about Saturday before I made those plans." Then he could take it to another level of honesty and say something like, "I was afraid you were condemning me, seeing me as someone who never listens to you and doesn't care about you having free time with your friend. So I overreacted."

- **When you find yourself arguing with your partner or withdrawing from her, take time to ask yourself if you may be experiencing underlying feelings like fear, shame, hurt, or self-doubt. At some point, when you are ready, risk openly expressing those feelings.**

By taking this approach Jason is exercising *open vulnerability*. He is choosing to be open and honest about his feelings and what he is actually experiencing in the moment. He is taking that risk to allow Cindy to see him as he is, both flawed and fragile. He is acknowledging that he has his imperfections and insecurities, just like the rest of us. He is being human. At first he may still be feeling some pain or discomfort inside, perhaps worrying how Cindy will react to what he reveals about himself, but he is on his way to discovering that risking openness leads to emotional strength and a stronger sense of himself.

It also opened a door in his relationship. From my clinical as well as personal experience, I have seen that women usually respond positively when their partner risks exposing his vulnerable feelings. Cindy might say something like, "I know you feel sensitive to being criticized by me." Then, with a new warmth and sense of connection, they could sit down and map out some plans for Sunday or for the following weekend that they both can agree to and feel good about.

But even if Cindy initially displays some lingering resentment about Jason's past behavior, he still can walk away feeling good about his willingness to be honest with himself and with Cindy. Why? Because he knows he has come clean, letting go of those painful, repressed feelings. He can begin to see that the security that comes from being real is *his*, no matter how his partner responds.

Jason also can see that he survived while revealing his deeper feelings that had been stuck underneath his critical, defensive posture. He might have been holding back before because of a fear that he could not tolerate the pain of speaking his most vulnerable truth, but he did it. In doing so, he discovered that those repressed feelings were much more painful over the long haul than the temporary discomfort of revealing himself. This recognition can encourage him to take further risks, revealing even more difficult and vulnerable feelings. For Jason, that might mean admitting that he feels threatened by a sense that Cindy is closer to her woman friend than to him.

In relating to Cindy, Jason also becomes stronger by reminding himself that even if he was "a rat" for failing to acknowledge how he had hurt Cindy in the past by his inconsiderate behavior, that was yesterday. What matters is now. This is critical for men to understand as they begin to access open vulnerability. Whatever you have done wrong before, whatever mistakes you've made in reacting to your partner's criticism, you have the capability of making a positive connection with her in the present. That, after all, is what matters most to her. When you listen to her, even while difficult feelings are triggered in you, she is likely to recognize it as a sign of caring. At the same time, *you* also recognize it as a sign of caring and that it took courage on your part.

To say, "I was wrong for having treated you that way before, and I'm sorry," you are showing in that moment that you are changing as a person because you have chosen a different response. So there's no need to beat yourself up inside. In fact, you are simply claiming your right to be that "flawed" human being. This all begins to build in you a quiet, inner strength. You begin to recognize that your willingness to be vulnerable really is something to be *proud* of!

Allowing your vulnerability to come through at any point during or after the heat of the battle also will help you feel much more relaxed in your relationship and stronger in your ability to handle the next conflicts with your partner that come along. Just stopping that cycle of having to defend yourself against your misdeeds and shortcomings brings an enormous sense of relief. A weight is lifted from your shoulders.

Dropping Your Facade

When a man accesses open vulnerability, as Jason did when he admitted to his mistake, he also is liberating himself from the powerful threat of his partner seeing through his façade. Often when your partner accuses you of having wronged her in some way, you are vulnerable in knowing that she sees the truth you want to hide. Perhaps you really were dishonest, inconsiderate, rejecting of her, or whatever it is she is pointing out, and you feel badly about it. Then, any complaint or displeasure she expresses will sound justified to you, no matter how hard you try to hide or deny it. Any time you try to hide something about yourself, it's a form of dishonesty. It also leaves you vulnerable in a way that creates an inner sense of weakness. You may be found out at any moment!

- **Keeping up a façade leaves you feeling on guard, drains your energy, and creates distance in your relationship. Letting down your guard ends that state of weakness that comes from hiding and allows your partner to respond to the real person you are.**

Keeping up a façade, of course, is a form of hidden vulnerability. It's the same corner that any of us back ourselves into when we try to impress someone that we are bigger than we actually perceive ourselves to be. It creates an underlying awareness of being false, with the anxiety of knowing that, like the Wizard of Oz bellowing into his microphone and blowing smoke, the curtain could be pulled on us at any time. Many people build themselves up like that when they are about to give a presentation or a performance in front of a group, as they yield to a desire to have the audience think they are more knowledgeable or more capable than they are. This heightens their performance anxiety. In a relationship, that kind of anxiety can be continuously tormenting because it seems like you're always "on stage."

Here's an example. Peter's partner Ellie tells him that the screen door is crooked and doesn't close right, and he assures her that he can fix it. Sounds fine, except that Peter doesn't know the first thing about fixing screen doors. But he does know that Ellie's father was a natural handyman around her house growing up and that she appears to highly value that ability in a man. He doesn't want to admit to her that he is severely deficient in this area, and it hasn't really come up in their relationship before. Now he's anxious that if

Ellie finds out how incapable he is with household repairs, she will think less of him and poke fun at him. So he keeps up the façade.

At first, that means delaying the project for days and then even weeks, constantly giving excuses why he can't get to it. Then he makes a clumsy attempt at fixing the screen door, but it only gets worse. Now he has to try to explain why it wasn't his fault. Then Ellie says she's going to invite her dad over to take care of it, and Peter insists there is no need for that. On and on the pretend game goes, until Ellie eventually catches on. When Peter gets found out, he feels a moment of rising fear. But Ellie assures him that she doesn't think any less of him as a man or love him any less. That was the real insecurity that drove him to put up his false front in the beginning. With that threat gone, he can finally drop his façade, but only after weeks of increased anxiety.

That kind of anxiety often becomes intensified for men in the sexual arena. If you feel concerned about proving yourself or living up to a certain image in bed, that will obstruct the natural flow of lovemaking.

Paradoxically, just becoming aware of your defensive efforts to protect a false image can bring you more in touch with your authentic core experience of yourself. If you understand *why* you have been trying to fool your partner into thinking you fit some image, you no longer need to do it. You may discover that you were only trying to convince yourself that you are a good person, a caring person, a loving person, or a capable person, while you were terrified of the possibility of your partner seeing that you aren't. But as you engage in open vulnerability and begin to own and share your limitations, insecurities, and selfishness, there is no balloon for anyone to puncture. You are released from that draining and depleting energy required to push something out of your own awareness and keep it hidden from others. The war inside you is over. You feel more at home with yourself, more rooted in your own shoes.

Something else happens when you make the shift to open vulnerability. If your partner is able to respond positively and show that she accepts and loves you for who you are, old wounds you have been carrying for years can be healed. For example, when Cindy shows love and acceptance for Jason when he admits to not taking her needs into consideration over those weekend plans, it opens the door for him to access feelings about his childhood. In Jason's childhood, he often would tell his parents about some new plan he was excited about, only to have them criticize his idea and question his wisdom. So, feeling hurt, he learned to keep all his plans to himself. Not surprisingly, that's just what he was doing with Cindy when he made plans without consulting her. Now that he sees the connection, he can begin to heal that old childhood pain.

With Peter, let's imagine that early on he had caught himself in his own "act" about the screen door and told Ellie of his insecurities. Imagine her laughing and telling him, "Sweetheart, you have much more important talents than fixing screen doors." That would have an enormously healing effect on Peter. It turns out that his own father used to criticize him constantly for ways in which he "wasn't being a man." Now Peter finds that over time, he can take a deeper plunge into open vulnerability and experience his sadness and anger over his childhood and adolescent experience. This allows him to let go of the wound more and more, and it helps him to empower himself to be the kind of person, and man, that he wants to be, not what he was told he must be.

Understanding a Man's Insecurity

It's important to understand that, like Peter, most men struggle more with vulnerability and intimacy because they grew up hearing advice like "Be a man" or "Act like a man." Such statements serve as ever-present reminders that being a man is an *achievement*, not a given. It's always in question. This creates a constant insecurity and leaves a man carrying an image of how he thinks he should act, especially around a woman.

Let's say your partner says she is busy and asks you to do the laundry. Instantly, you feel a conflict because, at least to some degree, you still believe that doing such household chores is unmanly. So you might refuse to do the laundry to protect your male image, but you feel guilty for letting your spouse down. Or you might do the laundry but resent having to perform an act that undermines your masculine role. So, until you become aware of those culturally imposed images and their crippling effect, you are likely to fall into hidden vulnerability with your partner.

Also, it's important to recognize that a man's unique experiences and conditioning creates a special vulnerability that shows up in all kinds of interactions with his partner. While women have their own challenges with intimacy, they don't come to the table with the same destructive limitations. Unlike men, women tend to accept the fact that they can be hurt by others. They are much more at home with feelings of inadequacy or weakness. In fact, they frequently connect with their women friends by sharing those very feelings. If a woman gets into a fight with her partner, she can go to her friends and receive caring, empathy, and understanding for having marital problems. Conversely, a man fears that if he dared to go to his male friends for support, they would get uncomfortable, make some crack like "That's just how women are," and quickly change the subject.

As we have already seen, when you feel hurt by someone, you see this as a sign of weakness. This puts you in a difficult dilemma when your partner does or says something that hurts you. You may feel not only the original pain from her complaint or criticism but also the further pain of seeing yourself as weak for feeling hurt and therefore less of a man. You have taken a double hit.

Something else happens. As you feel the shame of feeling hurt by your partner, you are likely to project that self-critical attitude about your weakness onto *her*. In other words, you assume she would naturally be critical of you for feeling hurt because she must share the same view that men are supposed to be strong and not easily hurt. So, of course, if you openly acknowledge your hurt, as Jason struggled to do, you believe you could be opening yourself to her judgment and ridicule, which would make you feel even worse. Also, you are convinced that she could exploit this vulnerability and use it as an opening to attack, which is how boys often react to other boys who show signs of weakness.

Clearly, when you feel hurt by your partner's disapproval but can't accept that feeling in yourself, you are caught in hidden vulnerability. In this state, you often try to override your hurt by becoming angry. If you're not expressing this anger by attacking your partner, you're probably clamming up and walking away. Refusing to talk about the issue in this way is called *stonewalling*, and it's a form of fighting back while protecting yourself. Sometimes men see this as their only option, especially if they don't want to get angry and defensive. But when you try to avoid hurtful feelings and self-critical thoughts this way, they get locked up inside. In this way, you are really stonewalling *yourself*. And when you remain emotionally blocked, you are incapable of real communication with your partner.

What the Woman Can Do:

For men, becoming aware of all their feelings and their impact on them is a major first step in eventually becoming vulnerable. It is, ultimately, their responsibility to find their way to open vulnerability and all its rewards. But it is also true that women's responses dramatically impact men's efforts, for better or for worse. So as a woman, you have choices. I will be walking you through some of those choices and illustrating how making the *wrong* choices can discourage his vulnerability, while making the *right* choices can encourage open vulnerability. But before I do, let's back up a moment.

We all know that in recent years we have been going through major transitions in sex roles. Women have been demanding equal rights in all aspects of life. But in any transition, there is a period of conflict between the desire for change and the conscious or unconscious holding onto the old and familiar. For example, most men may support the *idea* of equality in sharing household duties when both partners work full-time. Yet in practice, men generally do far less than fifty percent of the work at home. They are, to some extent, holding onto the old system.

Now consider that women today are demonstrating that they can be effective leaders in business and government, and that they can be forceful and tough when the situation requires it. At the same time, most women still allow themselves to feel weak, frightened, and vulnerable in their lives. They are finding a balance. In the quest for true equality, the question now becomes, can women allow and even encourage men to be sensitive and vulnerable as well as tough and forceful?

- **Real equality between women and men includes a man's right and need to be vulnerable, and your choices can either encourage or discourage his vulnerability in your relationship.**

Imagine a typical scenario. You feel that your partner has treated you in an uncaring manner, and you feel hurt and angry. You express this as directly as you can to him, but rather than listen empathically to you, he hears your words as an accusation. He responds defensively, and you feel unheard, invalidated, and further rejected.

Now you have a choice. You may find yourself interpreting his defensiveness as evidence that he's trying to protect his "male ego." You can conclude that he enjoys being on top and holding power over you. You can see him as a typical man, thoughtless and inconsiderate of your feelings. And you can respond to him with all the blaming or withdrawal that goes with this interpretation. But if you make that choice, you will certainly be discouraging his vulnerability. Any way that you hold onto a "strong man" image of him and see him as someone not readily threatened or hurt, someone who should always be available to respond to *your* needs and *your* feelings, you are colluding with him in his defensiveness.

Here's the other choice. Even though you may still feel angry and hurt, recognize that on his side there is pain underneath the verbal torrents he sends your way, and hurt behind his cloud of defensiveness. When he hears you tell him how he has been uncaring toward you, he may be experiencing acute shame, fear, or inadequacy. Recognize that through his social conditioning as a man, he is insecure about *not* being on top. Keep in mind the possibility that just because he isn't showing vulnerability doesn't mean he isn't feeling it. Remember how hidden vulnerability works. So you might say, "You seem angry. Tell me more about what's going on for you." You can acknowledge that what you've said may have hurt him.

- **If you suspect that he may be feeling wounded after a conflict with you, tell him that you understand how he may feel. Then, when he shows any sign of risking his vulnerability, urge him to tell you about it and show him your appreciation.**

Often just telling him that you understand how he may feel is all he has to hear from you to open the door to open vulnerability. But it's not always enough. Keep in mind the influences he received in growing up a male in our culture.

Because men often believe that having vulnerable feelings is a sign of weakness in itself, you can help him by making it clear that you consider these feelings natural and do not make him less of a man to you.

When you are seeking ways to help a man feel free enough to show his vulnerable feelings, sometimes you may find that you don't have to say anything at all. It often helps to just look at him with compassion, or perhaps touch his hand. These kinds of responses, like the others we have discussed, will encourage him to make the choices that will bring him closer to open vulnerability. You also need to understand that all these choices on how to relate to his struggles with vulnerability don't arise only in the conflicts in his relationship with you. Men hit the wall between hidden and open vulnerability regularly in response to all kinds of life situations, and you can help or hurt the cause of them becoming more open when it happens.

Let's say you notice that as he moves away from the dinner table he is holding his back stiffly. You're tempted to say something, but you remember how in the past he has appeared to resent your "making a fuss" over him and so you refrain. But that choice only colludes in his hidden vulnerability, where he may be feeling not only physical pain but also anxiety over what it could mean while telling himself to "suck it up." Instead of silence, you could choose to say to him, "I know you think your back stiffness is no big deal, but just lie down and let me rub it for you anyway." Then, while you're giving him that back rub, gently remind him that you know it's hard for him to ask for help but that you care very much about what's happening to him. Now you are encouraging open vulnerability.

Consider another common scenario. He has been struggling at work and fears that he could be fired or laid off, which could mean serious problems for your financial state. He drops an occasional hint about what's going on but appears to be guarding his vulnerability and trying to remain "strong" and not burden you with his "minor worries." You may be feeling anxious yourself about what may happen with his job, so to protect yourself against your own feelings you remain silent when he brings it up at all and wait for him to back off. Meanwhile, you keep telling yourself that "he will work it out by himself." In this way, you are colluding in his hidden vulnerability and making things worse.

The other choice is to assure him that it's very important for you to get the full picture of his work situation. Remind him that there is no need for him to take care of your feelings because you can do that yourself, and that if changes related to your finances become necessary you will work together with him to ease the crunch. It's true that making this choice may require you to drop your own possible avoidance of responsibility in money matters. If you do that, however, there's a much better chance that eventually he will share the truth about his fears and insecurities and look toward you for the empathy and emotional support he really needs.

- **As he tries to deal with his own personal issues, such as struggles at work or his fears about his health, take inventory of how you might be colluding in the way he hides his vulnerability because of your own lingering beliefs of what a man *should* be. Also, ask yourself whether you might be avoiding taking on equal responsibility for dealing with the problem confronting him.**

When he does share those difficult feelings with you, he is moving toward open vulnerability. At the same time, the two of you as a couple are beginning to experience that real equality that comes only when men and women both have the right to be recognized and accepted as strong yet vulnerable to being threatened or hurt by each other. As we have just seen, women can have a major influence on making this kind of *equality of vulnerability* a reality in their relationships. Still, men need to take it upon themselves to learn how to admit to having normal human feelings, to break free of the shame over being hurt and afraid so that they won't be paralyzed by hidden vulnerability. In my work with couples, I have witnessed profound changes when one or both partners are able to contribute to his efforts at being open. Here's one example.

Richard had to travel frequently for his business, and whenever he got ready to leave home, Laura would become distressed. The night before he was to leave for one three-day conference, Laura avoided talking to him and didn't sleep much. In the morning, she snaps, "Why do you have to go this time?" and proceeds to criticize him further. Richard mumbles, "We've been over this many times before" and goes back to reading the newspaper and shuffling through his conference schedule. As he slips out the door with only a perfunctory goodbye kiss, they both feel miserable. Richard knows intellectually that he is not at fault for needing to travel for his business, but he can't help feeling guilty about Laura's pain while also resenting how her criticism seems to be a way of trying to control him. But instead of confronting any of these feelings, he becomes distant.

As we explored these issues in couple's therapy, Richard revealed that his parents used to criticize him all the time. So part of the sting he felt from Laura's "jabs" came from the painful memories of his past. By tracing those old hurts to their roots and confronting his feelings toward his parents, Richard was able to work through his childhood wounds. Doing so enabled him to see Laura much differently. Over time, he felt less troubled by her criticism and less threatened by her responses to his trips away. He could see more clearly that he was not doing anything wrong, as he used to feel when his parents scolded him. He found he could now listen to her feelings.

Laura was impacted by old wounds of her own. She tapped into a fear of abandonment that she carried from the memory of her father leaving her family when she was only five years old. Each time Richard left, it triggered a fear that something might happen to him and, like her father, he would never come back. In stifling or minimizing those feelings, she was experiencing her own hidden vulnerability, and her critical posture toward Richard was contributing to his distancing. In couple's therapy she came to grips with her fears by recognizing their origin. Then she acknowledged responsibility for her own feelings and gave up blaming Richard.

For Richard, the change was especially dramatic and liberating. Part of his aloof behavior earlier stemmed from his belief that the only way to help Laura in her pain would be not to go away at all, and he knew he already had cut his travel to the bare minimum. Now he could see that he could take his business trips but still strongly support Laura, just by paying attention to her feelings about being left. Being openly vulnerable in acknowledging his pain from the criticism he experienced in childhood helped him to feel less threatened by her discomfort, which enabled him to tune into Laura's real and natural feelings.

The next time he went away, Richard was able to say to Laura, "I'm sorry. I know this is hard for you." He promised to call her as soon as he arrived and to call her at least once every day. As they shared a long goodbye hug, he felt better, more equal. Laura felt Richard's acceptance and love, which had the healing effect of greatly reducing her anxiety. Richard recognized that they both had vulnerable feelings, yet in that recognition he felt stronger in the relationship and stronger in himself.

The Feelings under Your Complaint

Like Laura, Angela was able to assist her partner Tom in letting go of his argumentative, defensive posture by practicing more open vulnerability herself. Tom was starting a new advertising business and wanted Angela to come in and lend her bookkeeping and personnel skills for a year or two to help him get off the ground, as she had done with one of his earlier businesses. She kept telling him that she didn't like doing the work that would be involved and that she wanted enough time for her own interests at home. He just kept arguing that he really needed her and called her selfish. Naturally, she accused him of not listening to her. They had reached an impasse, with hard feelings on both sides.

From many previous experiences with other couples, I knew that sometimes the woman accuses her partner of not being understanding of her when part of the problem is that she is not revealing *her* vulnerable feelings. So I suggested to Angela that she might not be getting to her deeper vulnerable feelings related to telling Tom "no" about working with him. Finally she admitted, "When I work for you in your business, I feel like I'm walking in your shadow." That was much riskier than simply saying she didn't like the work! Angela had exposed the painful feeling of not being her own person.

- **When you believe your partner is not being empathic toward you, ask yourself if part of the reason may be that you haven't expressed some of your own deeper and more vulnerable feelings. If so, risk sharing them with him.**

After Angela shared her deeper, more vulnerable feelings, it was Tom's turn to practice empathy. What if he didn't care about Angela's feelings? That would leave her feeling even more hurt and probably leave him in a state of hidden vulnerability. It took some effort, but eventually Tom was able to understand and accept Angela's strong need to do something that supported living her own life, rather than stifling herself to work for him. He responded empathically to her. More than that, he reached deeper for his own vulnerable feelings and realized that he was feeling anxious and insecure about this new venture and was hoping that Angela's support-ive presence would help him avoid those feelings. Once he faced the truth of his own vulnerability more openly, he began to see that he didn't need to depend on Angela to make him feel okay.

It's not easy for any of us to reach down and reveal more vulner-able feelings during a pattern of conflict in our relationship. As John Welwood writes in his helpful relationship guide *Journey of the Heart*, "The dream of love would have us believe that something is wrong if a relationship causes us pain. Yet trying to avoid the wound of love only creates a more permanent kind of damage. It prevents us from opening ourselves fully, and this keeps us from ever forming a deeply satisfying intimate connection."

Jonathan faced that kind of challenge in dealing with Sherry when he would come home after a very difficult day at work. Typi-cally, as he walked in the door he would mention that it had been an unpleasant day and then watch for her response. Sherry would casu-ally say something like, "Oh, sorry you had a rough day" and turn back to her dinner preparations. Though Jonathan really wanted to share more about his problems and dilemmas at work, he took her behavior as a message that she wanted him to leave it at that and so kept quiet. Inside, in his place of hidden vulnerability, he was afraid that if he showed more of his real pain or even asked for a hug, she would just put him down, which would hurt even worse than what he had been through at work. So he avoided that wound of love.

Let's consider the costs of that decision for Jonathan. First, he is suffering alone, not feeling love and support from his mate. Also, Jonathan's unwillingness to go further with his vulnerability was preventing Sherry from expressing her nurturing side, which not only could create more closeness and balance between them but also could boost *her* self-esteem. Even if Sherry still turned a cold shoul-der the first time Jonathan tried to reveal more, he might be able to kindle her caring feelings by saying, "Please put the frying pan down for a minute. I really need to talk about all this." In that way, he would be demonstrating that he really is vulnerable and really *needs* her, and chances are that she would respond with warmth and caring.

- **Expressing your deep need for your partner leaves you feeling much less alone. It also is likely to kindle an empathic and nurturing response, which is good for her and for your relationship.**

Even if Sherry did reject Jonathan to some degree while he was open about revealing how much he needed her, he still would gain. He would know he was being honest and that he was strong enough to openly face a degree of rejection.

For her part, Sherry could help by actively encouraging Jonathan's vulnerability from the start. Instead of brushing him off, she might admit that she also had a difficult day and that she needed to finish preparing dinner before she could focus on him. "I know you're having strong feelings about whatever happened to you and I want to talk about it later," she might say as she softly touches his arm. The resulting warmth between them would lead Jonathan toward really sharing those deeper feelings when they did talk later.

I know from my own experience how difficult it can be to admit to feelings that seem foolish, childish, or neurotic. My partner Carol recently went through a period in which she was productively busy with her creative writing. That meant that I needed to take on more of the household chores. Basically, I felt fine about that because I valued and wanted to support Carol's creative work. Yet while scrubbing those dishes I felt an inner discomfort that I just couldn't shake. As I dipped into this feeling, I had a sense of humiliation, or shame mixed with resentment. I felt bothered that for some time Carol had been leaving all the dishes for me to wash, like I was being put in the role of "designated dishwasher." I noticed a feeling of inferiority and found myself thinking that I was being treated like "the maid."

I felt conflicted and stuck. I worried that if I complained or expressed my resentment, Carol would just get angry. I imagined her arguing that she usually did most of the housework even though she also worked outside the home. I pictured her telling me how inconsiderate I was acting in not giving her support when she needed it, especially after all the ways she has supported me. I figured she would be right in saying all that, so my feelings could well be irrational and unjustified. Also, I wondered if I was falling into old conditioned ideas that being the dishwasher was unmasculine. Was I experiencing the dread of being what was called in my youth a "henpecked husband?"

What was I to do? I didn't know if my feelings were objectively realistic or justified. Yet they were there and I couldn't escape them. I knew that if I kept these feelings to myself that it would have negative consequences on me *and* on my relationship with Carol. I recognized that self-critical thoughts that I was being inconsiderate and unfair, perhaps childish, were weakening to me, and that if I tried to hide my shame and resentment I would go into a shell and become distant from Carol. I saw there was no choice, or at least no constructive choice, except to treat my feelings as legitimate whether or not they were rational or fair and to be open with my partner about them.

When I expressed these feelings to Carol without claiming that I was *right* and she was wrong, she was able to listen to them without becoming defensive. So my open vulnerability led to being able to receive empathy from Carol.

- **It's okay to acknowledge feelings that you may consider irrational, unfair, or even childlike. It helps to begin by making it clear that you are not claiming that your feelings are necessarily realistic or justified.**

As it turned out, Carol also agreed to do at least some work on the dishes even while concentrating on her writing, so I gained there, too! We had arrived at a solution through the process in which each of us, starting with me, recognized the legitimacy of our feelings, even if they seemed totally irrational. We also understood the critical need for each partner to access that place of vulnerability.

For a man especially, vulnerability becomes a source of strength through risking, practicing, and self-acceptance. When you are able to accept and thus integrate aspects of yourself and vulnerable feelings that you had disowned, you become more whole. You begin to experience the difference between selling yourself on the idea that you are a good, worthwhile person and the grounded sense that you are who you are, warts and all, and that's okay. Instead of trying to boost yourself, or defend yourself while denying your frailties and limitations, you accept them with compassion. Then, when you are forced to face aspects of yourself you may dislike or are ashamed of, especially when your partner is confronting you or rejecting you, that threat or hurt is less devastating because of your overall belief that you are an acceptable human being.

Summary Guidelines

For the Man:

1.   Admitting that your partner can hurt you by her actions and words just means you are human. It makes you vulnerable, and allowing yourself to be vulnerable in that way is an act of strength. It means you're willing to really engage in an intimate relationship, which is something for you to be proud of while enabling her to feel cared for.

2.   When you find yourself arguing with your partner or withdrawing from her, take time to ask yourself if you may be expe-

riencing underlying feelings like fear, shame, hurt, or self-doubt. Risk openly expressing those feelings, recognizing that she will likely be receptive to that.

3. Keeping up a façade leaves you feeling on guard, drains your energy, and creates distance in your relationship. Letting down your guard ends that state of weakness that comes from hiding and allows your partner to respond to the real person you are.

4. Asserting your right to have human sensitivities and fears is a way of standing up for yourself. There is strength in that.

5. Expressing your deep need for your partner leaves you feeling much less alone. It also is likely to kindle an empathic and nurturing response, which is good for her and for your relationship.

6. It's okay to acknowledge feelings that you may consider irrational, unfair, or even childlike. It helps to begin by making it clear that you are not claiming that your feelings are necessarily realistic or justified.

For the Woman:

1. Real equality between women and men includes a man's equal right and need to be vulnerable, and your choices can either encourage or discourage his vulnerability in your relationship.

2. If you suspect that he may be feeling wounded after a conflict with you, tell him that you understand how he may feel. Then, when he shows any signs of risking his vulnerability, urge him to tell you about it and show him your appreciation.

3. Because men often believe that having vulnerable feelings is a sign of weakness in itself, you can help him by making it clear that you consider those feelings natural and do not make him less of a man to you.

4. As he tries to deal with his own personal issues, such as his struggles at work or his fears about his health, take inventory of how you might be colluding in the way he hides his vulnerability because of your own lingering beliefs of what a man *should* be. Also, ask yourself whether you might be avoiding taking on equal responsibility for dealing with the problem confronting him.

5. When you believe your partner is not being empathic toward you, ask yourself if part of the reason may be that you haven't expressed some of your own deeper and more vulnerable feelings. If so, risk sharing them with him.

3

Don't Try to Fix It

Men who may want to practice empathy in their relationship face another major hurdle that comes from ingrained behavior. That is, when men are faced with a problem they tend to focus on action. They want to fix it, and the sooner the better! If they are having a difficult time with something or a painful feeling, they want to do something to solve the problem and/or get rid of the pain. If their partner is having a problem, they want to show her what she can do to solve it. This approach works fine in lots of situations, but in the realm of relationships, especially intimate relationships, it is often a complete failure. Here's an example.

David and Ann had been living together for eight years. When Ann said that she wanted to split up, David did not object. He told her he thought it was a good idea for both of them, and then he quickly got involved with another woman. This new relationship seemed ideal in many ways, yet he was unable to fully invest in it. He found himself lacking energy and enthusiasm in his work and toward life in general. Finally, he had to admit that he was depressed. At least David did not turn to alcohol as many men do when they are depressed. When he came to see me he had a vague idea that his depression must have something to do with the ending of his relationship with Ann. Yet he insisted that he had no strong feelings about the break-up.

With work, David came to see over time how he was protecting himself in two ways: first, by convincing himself that he wasn't upset by the break-up, and second by jumping into a new relationship. When I questioned him further I learned that whenever he got into a painful interaction with Ann, he would bury his feelings and fantasize leaving her and being with another woman. Both his fantasies and his behavior reflected his life-long pattern of using action to avoid painful feelings.

This time David realized that his escapist defenses were not working and that he had to do something different. I was able to convince him to try an approach that was radical and unfamiliar to him: let go of his action-oriented search for solutions and simply drop down into his feelings about his break-up with Ann. When he did that he got in touch with intense hurt and sadness along with anger toward Ann for leaving him. That opened the door for him to do the necessary grieving in a short period of time and his acute depression lifted. The key that enabled him to do that was his willingness to be still and tune in to his feelings rather than *doing* something to change them. Of course, while he was no longer depressed he was still left with sadness and regret that he had not been more open with Ann.

What would have happened if David had not been so ready to agree with the idea of splitting up? What would have happened if at some point he had told Ann how much her leaving hurt him? She may have interpreted his non-objection to her suggestion of separating as confirmation that he didn't feel much for her. It is possible that if he had been in touch with and shown her his feelings of hurt and sadness she would have felt different about the relationship. Maybe she even would not have felt the need to leave. It is also possible that their relationship would have been better all along if he hadn't turned to action-oriented fantasies of finding another woman whenever they got into emotional difficulties. Their chance of emotional understanding and connection was lost both early on and at the end.

• **Don't jump to an action solution when facing emotional problems with your partner. It will block awareness of your feelings and your ability to empathize with her. Actions, if needed, can come later.**

It is not easy to know for sure whether there was anything Ann could have done to break through David's defensive wall. In most relationships, however, there are things women can do long before they reach the break-up point Ann and David had come to. For one thing, don't assume that if a man shows no feeling about even the possibility of ending your relationship that he has little feeling for you. It may simply be that he is very good at hiding feelings from himself and from you. Be open to the possibility that he would only discover those feelings when he is faced with the reality of living without you. That often happens with men. And if his becoming more aware of his emotional attachment to you does make you feel differently about leaving, strongly suggest couples counseling. There may be room to work it out and build a stronger relationship.

The tendency for men to do something to escape from feelings often shows up in the sexual arena. For example, if you as a man are feeling threatened by her disapproval or rejection, you could turn to sex for reassurance. You may just be experiencing a lack of closeness with her and you try to bridge the gap through sexual love. Or you could be feeling weak and inadequate, so you use sex to boost your sense of masculinity. Maybe something happened that upset you and you are looking for sexual pleasure to make yourself feel better.

That's how it was for James in his relationship with Helen. James had just been through a painful disappointment at work. The promotion that he expected was given to somebody else. He felt hurt and depressed and found himself doubting his competence. When he got home he did what lots of men do. He tried to escape from his feelings by sticking his nose in the newspaper and turning on the TV. He said nothing about it to Helen. Later that night he tried "lovemaking." It didn't work. Helen could tell that James was distracted and that he had some agenda other than being involved with her. Not surprisingly, she was emotionally and sexually unresponsive. She was also hurt and angry, feeling that she was being used. What was supposed to make James feel better ended up in his feeling worse. He was wounded again.

- **Using sex to compensate for your real feelings doesn't work, and it may have a negative effect on your relationship.**

What the Woman Can Do:

If your partner proposes sex after he has been distant or preoccupied, suggest talking first, perhaps sharing the events of the day. If you begin lovemaking, and it's not working because he seems distracted and not emotionally with you, try talking then. Treat it as a normal thing that happens at times. If you are feeling upset, you may need to postpone talking about it until later. Avoid treating it as a failure or as if something is wrong. Ask him if he has things on his mind that may be distracting him. Talk about yourself, your need for emotional contact, and how that is part of your sexual responsiveness. Of course, if you are feeling hurt or angry or other feelings, you need to express that as well. Since sex is such a highly charged area, it is important that you do not criticize him or imply that there is something wrong with him for not being like you.

I'll share a tragic example of a man's tendency to focus on action instead of being open to his feelings as it relates to a couple I knew personally. Dennis and Betty were both devastated by the loss of their eight-year-old daughter in an automobile accident. Dennis reacted by getting busily involved in dealing with practical matters—trying to fix things. First, he took care of all the funeral arrangements. Later, he made special efforts to encourage social contacts, arranged trips, and did everything he could think of to try to make Betty more comfortable and feel less pain.

The problem is that he kept *his own* feelings in check. The result was that while Betty appreciated Dennis's taking care of the practical things, she felt totally alone in her grief. She felt estranged from her partner at a time when she needed him most. In his effort to escape from or reduce his wife's pain and his own, Dennis was preventing a deeper healing for both of them. She needed the empathic connection more than his comforting and care-taking. Also, he deprived himself of his own need to grieve fully, and he deprived himself and Betty of the opportunity for a deeper closeness that can come from sharing a mutual pain. They needed each other, and when they were not able to empathically come together their relationship suffered. They grew further and further apart, and eventually they divorced. Sadly, it ended as a double loss.

- **When something troubling affects both of you, share the pain. That brings you together when it is most needed.**

What the Woman Can Do:

If you and your partner are facing mutual troubles, here's the first step. Check to see if you are getting caught in your own need to be taken care of and colluding in your partner's focusing on you, and thus avoiding his own feelings. Let him know that while you appreciate his attention and care-taking, it is not necessary, and that you have a much deeper need to have him share his feelings so that you can join each other. You may have to say that in different ways and repeat it several times.

Because of our tendency to focus on action, we men often project that bias on to our women partners. When she complains about something we are doing, we make the mistake of thinking that the only thing that will satisfy her will be for us to completely change our behavior. And if it involves giving up or changing something that is important to us, her complaint can be very threatening, sure to trigger defensiveness.

Glen and Doris had the same fight practically every weekend. Glen wanted to spend half of most weekends away from home playing music with his musician friends. Doris wanted him to spend the bulk of the weekend at home with her. He accused her of being too dependent, relying on him to meet all of her needs for companionship and entertainment. She accused him of not caring about her. At some point, I suggested that Glen put aside all his feelings and opinions about fairness and right or wrong, including his thoughts about solving the problem. The idea was for him to have no agenda except to listen to Doris in order to grasp how she felt. Doris's job was to limit herself to expressing only her feelings. They both understood that they would each have a turn in doing this.

The more Doris talked, with Glen doing nothing but listening, the more open she became. She began by explaining how much she liked being with him and how important his company was to her. Then, with lots of feeling, she described how painfully lonely she felt when he was not with her on weekends. Once she completed saying all of that and felt listened to, she was able and willing to take the next step and "tell on herself." She admitted that she was somewhat over-reliant on Glen for companionship and agreed that she tended to be socially inhibited, which she attributed to being unsure of herself. That was a basic turning point in their communication. Glen felt greatly relieved that Doris was not putting all the blame on *him*. His feelings of guilt and defensiveness had vanished, and he was able to sincerely say that he was sorry that she felt lonely when he was gone on weekends. This had a dramatic effect on Doris. Feeling Glen's caring, she softened. Then she was able to put aside her own agenda and genuinely listen to Glen when he spoke about his music. When Glen saw that she was fully present to listen to him, he felt safe in sharing with her the deep meaning that his music had for him.

What happened next? There was very little change, at least directly in their behavior. Glen did not give up his weekend music, yet they both felt much better about it. This is another example of the power of empathic listening. As long as they both believed that the solution was totally in the realm of action—the man's approach—they were stuck. Glen couldn't listen empathically to Doris since he was afraid that the only thing that would satisfy her would be his giving up his music. Doris couldn't listen as long as she believed that the only thing that would make her feel better would be for Glen to stay at home with her for most of the time on weekends. As it worked out, Glen continued most of his weekend music, with Doris joining him occasionally. While Doris missed him when he was gone, they both felt understood and cared about, and it was no longer a divisive issue.

- **Expressing feelings and having those feelings understood and accepted is often sufficient in itself, and it may not be necessary to change behavior.**

Sometimes, what appears to be merely expressing your feelings is really an attempt to get your partner to behave differently. It is actually a form of manipulation. Here's how it looked with one couple I worked with.

Gregory and Dolores were continuing a dispute that had gone on for months, while becoming more and more destructive. Gregory often made sarcastic or critical comments about Dolores's involvement in all the activities that took her away from home. Dolores felt that she was doing things that were very important to her and that she was coming out into the world in a growing, creative way. She didn't like his judgmental cracks and felt that he was being self-centered and dependent with no regard for her feelings and needs. Their relationship was in serious jeopardy. Finally, Gregory reached the point where he knew he had to do something different. He decided to risk letting his guard down and say what he really felt underneath his critical cracks. He got up his courage and said, "I'm afraid you'll find somebody else."

Suddenly, everything changed. Feeling deeply moved, Dolores reached out and touched Gregory. In an instant, the anger, the hurt and the wall between them was gone. They were connected again—their love was back. From that place, they were able to constructively work on the problem in a way that gave full consideration to each person's needs.

The error that Gregory made in the beginning was to treat the situation from the point of view of action. It was something that he didn't like that he was going to fix, in this situation by being critical and hoping to influence Dolores to change her behavior. When this tactic didn't work he was forced to face the fact that it was not a situation that he could control. It was out of the action solution mode, and he knew he was helpless. That was scary and painful for Gregory. Yet, once he accepted the fact that he couldn't make her change her behavior, he was able to access the more vulnerable feeling of fear of losing her. If he had done that early on and expressed those underlying feelings he could have saved them both from months of painful disruption.

- **Give up the illusion of being able to control your partner's behavior. That will make it easier for you to access the feelings that you need to experience and express.**

When your partner is being critical or controlling you may need to begin by expressing your feelings and standing up for yourself. After you have done that, see if you can find out what his underlying, more vulnerable feelings are. Is he feeling hurt or threatened or humiliated by your behavior? You could ask him what he is feeling under the surface. And if your asking doesn't yield anything, you could speculate out loud what you think he may be feeling and not expressing.

One common way that a man gets in trouble with his partner emerges when she tells him about a problem she is having with someone and he comes up with a solution. Let's look at a typical situation and see if you recognize yourself. She tells you a story about an incident at work in which she felt rebuffed by a coworker. From your "fix it" orientation, you make suggestions of things she could say or do that would change the way she relates to this person. You're sure that these ideas will help her resolve the situation or make her feel better. Then you're frustrated when she doesn't even listen to your great ideas. Instead of appreciating your suggestions, she gets irritated with you.

What is going on? You try to help and this is the response you get? You are baffled and hurt. So why did she react that way? In the first place, she may have already considered the options you raised and could be taking your suggestions as superficial and making light of the dilemma that she feels that she is in. She may feel that you are treating her as if she is foolish or irrational. But these are not the main issues. The real issue is that advice and suggestions are *not* the primary thing that she wants. Nine times out of ten, her goal is not for you to tell her what to do, even though it may look that way when she tells you about the problem. More likely, what she wants is for you to understand her feelings and her situation as she perceives it. In other words, she just wants you to listen to her and be empathic. That's how she can feel connected with you and that's what she cares most about. Later, after she feels your presence and connection, she may be interested in your ideas to help the problem.

So before you rush in with your best solutions, try to ask her if that's what she wants before you offer it.

- **If your partner tells you about a problem she is having with someone, just listen empathically. Don't tell her what to do unless she asks for suggestions.**

Why Negotiation May Not Work

Here's another side to the fix-it approach that usually doesn't help in a relationship, a situation where both the man and the woman often wind up following a misguided strategy. It happens when the man and the woman face conflicting needs and wishes and quickly decide that the best thing to do is to discuss it and work out a solution together. And if there are painful feelings involved, they want to resolve it now. So they're both caught trying to fix it.

For example, let's say your partner wants to spend Christmas with her parents and you want to stay home. Or you want to buy a new car and she wants to use the money to paint and fix up the house. Or she wants you to work around the house on Saturdays and you want to spend Saturdays playing golf with your friends.

Faced with these kinds of dilemmas, both of you may be committed to the belief that you are intelligent, fair-minded people who should be able to talk things over and work out your differences. "I'll listen to your side and you'll listen to mine, and we will negotiate a solution that is considerate of both of us."

Unfortunately, while this approach works sometimes, often it does not work at all. And it is especially difficult when there are strong feelings on both sides. Why? Because your natural approach is to present a case in your behalf. While you listen to your partner, trying to be considerate, what you're mainly doing is figuring out how you're going to convince her to understand and accept *your* feelings and needs. You may try to shift from looking at the situation from your point of view to hers, while under the surface you are experiencing lots of unspoken questions: Who is right? What is fair? What is reasonable? Whose needs take preference? Who is being considerate, and who is being inconsiderate? Am I being taken advantage of? Who is in charge?

Here's the rub: All these questions, and the feelings attached to these questions, are obstructions that prevent real listening. You have an agenda, including the agenda to work out a solution. Your agenda gets in the way of total listening, and you know that your partner's listening is compromised by her agenda. Neither of you trusts that you will be fully, empathically listened to. Despite your best intentions, your guardedness is going to be there to some degree. The result is that you don't feel safe enough to access your most sensitive feelings, much less express them.

How can you get out of this seemingly impossible dilemma? The answer is doing something that may seem to make no sense at all. You need to completely step out of the fix-it mode, to put aside problem solving, and instead adopt a different goal. That goal is to listen with the sole purpose of *getting to know your partner better.* I admit that this is not easy. It means really listening, with no judgment and no motive except to understand your partner. It means that you are willing to live with the emotional pain of an unsolved relationship problem in the hopes that this new approach will yield results in the future.

When couples who have been at an impasse take this step, or even when one member of a couple makes this choice, something changes. One or both of you experiences being genuinely listened to, and feels validated and accepted for who you are. You feel known and cared for. It is a basic shift, and it is very powerful. Usually, when one person feels fully listened to, he or she is able to really listen to his or her partner, so it becomes a mutual process. The conflict hasn't been directly addressed, but the *relationship* has changed, and that changes everything. What was a problem before may seem to be virtually gone. Or the conflict is still there, with decisions still needing to be made, but the feelings around the conflict are different. Now there is a softness and openness between you that makes it much easier to resolve the problem.

• **When you are stuck in a conflict with your partner, give up negotiation and make as your only goal to listen in order to get to know your partner better. Once you have done that, ask your partner to listen to you in the same way. Decisions and negotiations, if necessary, can come later.**

An Exercise in Listening to Simply Understand

This exercise can be helpful in dealing with ongoing conflicts or in times when you have no pressing issues to resolve at all. Again, the goal is to understand, not to fix or change anything.

Take five minutes for one person to speak and the other person to listen. The goal of the speaker is to help your partner get to know you better. That means telling your partner your feelings, your thoughts, your concerns, your hopes, your dreams, etc., whatever you care most about communicating at the time. The job of the listener is to be silent and to speak only if you are unclear and need to ask for clarification.

After the five minutes are up, take a brief pause, enough to absorb the experience. Then switch roles. When each person has had the chance to speak and be listened to, move on to an open discussion. What did you learn about yourself and your partner? How open were you in disclosing to your partner? What did you hold back? How successful were you in just listening without an agenda? To what extent were your own feelings and judgments coming into play?

This is an exercise you may want to repeat several times. Each time you do it, see if you are willing to risk being more open in both your disclosure and your listening.

Summary Guidelines

For the Man:

1. Be aware of your tendency to look for an action solution when painful feelings come up in your relationship. Try just sitting with the feelings and sharing them with your partner when you are ready.

2. Check when you get interested in sex with your partner to see if there is some other feeling or need under the surface that is contributing to your wanting sex at that particular time. It doesn't work to avoid the underlying feelings, and it could have a negative effect on your "love-making" and the relationship.

3. When something disturbing happens to both of you, don't just be a care-taker. Share your feelings. You need each other.

4. When your partner wants you to stop doing something that you like doing, don't pick up the gauntlet and argue your case. Take time to listen with the only goal being to understand her feelings. Remember, fully grasping and respecting your partner's feelings and needs may be all or most of what is required.

5. Recognize that essentially you don't have the power to make your partner change her behavior. Instead, just tell her your feelings—how her behavior affects you. That may take courage, since it involves accepting your helplessness and vulnerability.

6. If your partner tells you about a problem she is having with someone, avoid coming up with practical solutions. Instead, try to understand her situation and feelings. If practical suggestions occur to you, ask her if that's what she wants.

7. Recognize that no matter how reasonable and fair couples try to be, negotiation of conflicts may not work. Try changing the goal to getting to know each other better.

For the Woman:

1. Encourage your partner to talk about his work and perhaps other activities outside the home. When he tells you about events, ask about his feelings, being careful to avoid pressuring or badgering.

2. When "love-making" is not working because your partner seems distracted and not emotionally with you, try discussing it at the time or later. Ask him if there may be things on his mind that may be bothering or worrying him.

3. When something troubling affects you both, let him know that you don't just want him to take care of you. Tell him that you need to join him by both of you sharing your feelings.

4. If your partner is criticizing or trying to control your behavior, try to get him to express the underlying feelings that are troubling him.

5. There are times that you may have to remind your partner that you don't want him to solve your problem, that you just want him to listen.

4

Let Go of Being "Right"

Question: "Do you want to be right or do you want your relationship?" Pause…. "Well?".… "I'm thinking."

I am amazed how often people, especially men, seem to be so attached to being right that they are unable to see and come to terms with the fact that their righteousness could not just be undermining the possibility of being empathic but even destroying their relationship!

Several factors contribute to men's need to be objectively right. As we discussed in Chapter 2, we men have learned to hold our feelings in, and to avoid showing sensitivity or neediness. Also, we have learned to put a great deal of value on being rational and logical. Finally, we have grown up learning the importance of winning, and especially making sure we are not on the losing end. When we put those factors together—non-expression of feelings, the need to be rational, and the importance of winning—we can see how that leads to putting a lot of emphasis on "right and wrong" in our interactions with our partners.

In Chapter 1, I described an incident in which Michelle accused Charlie of ignoring her at the previous night's party. Charlie's immediate response was to focus on the facts, coming up with examples of time he spent with her, to prove that she was wrong. Not only was Charlie being defensive, he was also doing the common male thing of focusing on the "objective facts." In so doing, he was not in touch with her feelings, and, at the same time, it served to keep him away from his own feelings. There was no empathic connection. When he finally put aside the "facts" and just listened empathically to Michelle, he was able to see the whole situation in a way that included feelings, hers and his. That opened him to the realization of what he had been hiding from himself: that he had been feeling emotionally distant from Michelle, including at the party.

Once he had taken that step, he could see that Michelle was right, that he had actually ignored her, though it was not easy to admit that. The so-called objective facts, supporting his claim that he had spent lots of time with Michelle, seemed superficial and irrelevant. Paradoxically, by letting go of his attachment to facts he was able to see the "facts" in a totally new way. This is a good example of how awareness of your feelings can enable you to see reality more deeply and clearly.

- **When you are facing a dispute with your partner, put the "facts" aside so that you can focus on the validity of her feelings and also your feelings. You may find that the facts themselves will come out looking different.**

Another way couples put up barriers to empathy is by being judgmental. And it is amazing how frequently people are unaware that they are being judgmental. As much as you believe that you are just stating "the facts," a statement like, "The house is a mess" is clearly judgmental. Whereas, if you speak for your feelings instead of an overt or implied judgment about the other person, you might say, "I feel upset when I see disorder and clutter and I can't relax." Another example of being judgmental would be asking, "Why didn't you call and let me know you were coming home late?" A non-judgmental alternative would be to say something like, "When you are not home at the time you said you would be home I get anxious and worried." The difference between the judgmental and the non-judgmental statements is that in the non-judgmental statement the emphasis is on *your* feelings and *your* reactions, not your partner's behavior.

When your partner is on the receiving end of those kinds of judgmental statements, she is almost certain to feel criticized and/or controlled and will probably react by becoming resentful and defensive. Each time this happens there is an accumulation of hurt and resentment that has a toxic effect on your relationship. She is likely to feel less and less like caring for you and giving you what you want. Even if she did give in to you out of a sense of pressure or intimidation, you would get a half-hearted compliance with an underlying resentment that would come out in other ways. It is also likely that she would protect herself by becoming generally more distant.

It is sad to see how often people, men in particular, defeat themselves by expressing their feelings and needs in a judgmental way. And since they don't see that they are being judgmental, they don't understand their partner's defensive reaction.

Of course, as a man you may notice that being judgmental may appear to have its payoff. You get a comfortable sense of being right, with reality and justice on your side. You might even feel intellectually and morally superior. But the biggest payoff is that by not putting your feelings out there, you are protected. This brings us to a crucial choice that we all face in our intimate relationships. If you give up trying to be right and tossing judgmental remarks, instead telling your partner how she is hurting you or what you need from her, you are taking a risk, sometimes a huge risk. You may discover the devastating truth that she doesn't care about your feelings and needs. Even though you may know better rationally, the underlying fear is still there.

What can help is to understand that feelings have little to do with rationality. The previously described interaction between Dolores and Gregory illustrates this well. Gregory felt very threatened by Dolores's involvement in activities outside the home. He couldn't bring himself to face and express his fear that she would find someone else and leave him. For months, he made all sorts of derogatory cracks about the things she was doing to the point that their relationship was in serious jeopardy. When he finally revealed the secret of his fears, everything changed. She responded by reaching out to him, and the disruptive, painful barrier was dissolved.

- **Being judgmental with your partner is self-protective. You're not showing yourself. It may be based on the fear that if you just openly show your feelings and needs she won't care.**

Let me share an example of how partners in a relationship often don't realize when they are being judgmental. Peter was anxious about Beverly's increase in drinking, knowing that she had a problem with alcoholism in the past. He was relieved when she decided to go to an AA meeting. When she came home she said that she was only going to go to certain select meetings and was not going to fully enter the 12-step program. When Peter heard this, he felt afraid that she was making a mistake, that she was avoiding facing her problem. At the same time, from past experience he knew the pitfalls of being judgmental and telling her what to do. He cautiously questioned her about her decision, suggesting that she may not get the benefit she needed if she didn't fully enter into the program. He felt confident that he was "right" in his assessment.

Did it work? Well, Beverly did listen calmly and politely, acknowledging that Peter had a legitimate point. Then she withdrew and was distant from him for several days. Peter was left wondering what he had done "wrong."

As I explored this problem with Peter and Beverly, we learned that she experienced his questioning as if he was still taking the role of the authority, the one who knew what was right for her. She felt diminished, as if he was treating her like a child. While she recognized that he was not being grossly judgmental, as he had been in the past, and she did appreciate that he was trying to help her, she was still hurt and angry that he lacked confidence in her. So she pulled away. If that same exchange had occurred with another couple there may have been no problem. A different woman may have taken Peter's comments as helpful suggestions from an equal partner. But given Beverly's sensitivity about being told what to do, combined with Peter's tendency to take the role of "the one who knows what's right," there was a problem for them.

This example shows how you can make a sincere effort to be non-judgmental and not succeed. It is possible that no matter what Peter had said, Beverly would have felt judged. Still, he could have done a better job on his end. How?

Let's imagine that instead of questioning Beverly's choice he simply said what he was feeling. So when she said what she planned to do about the AA meetings, he could have said something like, "That scares me. I really don't want alcohol to rule our lives as it did in the past." That would have made it easier for her to see that Peter was talking about *his* fears and not just acting like an authority, telling her what is right for her. Even if she didn't see that, Peter would have had the solid sense of knowing that he was showing his own feelings and not taking the parental role as she often accused him of doing.

- **When you genuinely speak for your feelings you can take comfort in knowing that you are not imposing your judgmental authority on your partner.**

We have been focusing on Peter in the above exchange, but of course that's only half the story. Beverly's behavior was also part of their "dance." Under the surface, she knew she was avoiding taking full responsibility for her alcoholism and need for help. On some level, she knew that Peter would not agree with her choice to only partly enter the AA program. While she probably didn't realize it, she was setting him up to be authoritative and tell her that she was doing the wrong thing. While she acknowledged that he was behaving in a less judgmental way than in the past, she still felt that he was clinging to the authority role in not trusting her judgment. What she failed to see, and later discovered, was that she was avoiding taking adult responsibility for her behavior and that, at least unconsciously, she wanted *him* to provide parental guidance.

- **When you are on the receiving end of judgmental comments, check yourself to see if you are avoiding responsibility in some way and drawing your partner into the position of authority.**

Judgmentalness can be especially hard for couples to recognize and deal with when it is expressed in subtle ways. It could come across in a tone of voice, a facial expression, a gesture. I'll use another situation with Beverly and Peter as an example. Beverly had become actively involved in artistic projects. Peter felt left out and was hurting. He knew he had to express his feelings to Beverly. Later, Peter assured me that he spoke to Beverly in a way that was not the least bit judgmental, yet she *still* reacted defensively. He told her, "You're doing all these different things and I feel like I'm not part of your life." When I heard that, I detected a complaining quality in his voice, and I pointed that out to him. He was able to see that and recognized that there was a judgmental aspect in his complaining manner. It was as if he were telling Beverly that she was doing something wrong, that she was being unfair to him.

At this point, I asked Peter to imagine that he told her in a non-complaining tone, "I'm *missing* you. I feel like I'm not part of your life and that *hurts* me." When he heard my suggestion, Peter said, "That would be putting my *heart* out there and it could be trampled on." I nodded. Peter had just touched upon what lots of men feel but never say. Seeing the intensity of his feelings and his self-protection made a big difference. It enabled him to recognize and understand why it was so hard for him to let go of the judgmental role. Once he had that awareness, he was able to do a much better job of dropping his authority role and relating to Beverly as an equal partner.

- **Judgmentalness is often expressed subtly and non-verbally. Check yourself to see if you may be implying that your partner is doing something wrong.**

When you speak for yourself and for your own feelings, you not only avoid the negative effects of being judgmental, but there is also much to be gained. Speaking about your own feelings gives a positive message. You are saying to her that if I show you my hurt or distress, I expect that you will care, even if it doesn't necessarily mean that you will change your behavior. It is complimentary to her, and it is treating yourself respectfully as someone deserving to be cared about.

Here's something else that many men especially are unaware of: asking to be cared for tends to kindle a caring response in your partner. Besides, it gives her the gift of being able to express the supportive, nurturing side of herself. And when you openly show your feelings and needs without any form of demanding or controlling, you are giving yourself the precious opportunity to be known and accepted by the central person in your life. This opens the door to healing old wounds and the personal growth that comes with that.

It's a way for you and your partner to be intimate and to grow together.

Speaking for I

A well known practice that can help you avoid being judgmental is called "speaking for I." You begin relevant statements with "I feel," "I want," "I think," etc. This may seem forced and awkward, especially at first, but over time you will see that it really does help to be more attuned to the experience of merely disclosing your feelings without any implication that somebody is "right" and somebody is "wrong."

Speaking for I can be very effective, but only if it is a sincere effort to speak about yourself. Your goal is simply that your partner understand your feelings and your needs. Of course, behind that is the hope and assumption that your feelings and needs matter to her. Unfortunately, people often use the "speaking for I" language in a way that is not honest self-disclosure. An example of pseudo "speaking for I" might be, "I feel that you're not being fair." In that example, you are starting with the words "I feel," but you're talking about the other person, not yourself. If you follow the real spirit of "speaking for I," you might say, "I think you are not being fair and I am angry about it." Any statement that begins with the words, "I feel that you" is obviously a comment about the other person, not yourself, and it violates the purpose of the practice. It impinges on the absurdity of saying, "I'm expressing my feeling, and I feel that you are wrong."

Another way that couples get caught in the mire of right and wrong is by trying to *explain* their feelings instead of simply sharing them. What if Gregory had given reasons for his fear that Dolores will find somebody else? He could have said things like, "You tell me how much you like Robert." "You go to lunch with Jim and you enjoy talking with him on the phone." To Gregory, his explanation would be a justification for his feelings. It's a way of stating that there is nothing screwed up or neurotic about him, that his fears are perfectly normal and reasonable. The effect of that would be implying that Dolores is doing something wrong, which, of course, would make her defensive, and it would have sabotaged the empathic connection that actually occurred. A helpful technique: if you catch yourself explaining your feelings, stop, take a breath, and try saying what you feel in one word.

- **Be careful about explaining your feelings. If your explaining is meant to justify, you are getting into the "right and wrong" trap. Avoid it.**

We can never be totally free of judgmentalness, of course. It will happen sometimes, maybe subtly, despite our best efforts. Perhaps the best we can do is try to catch ourselves either when it happens or later when we have had the chance to think about it. Then start over and try to get it right. The important thing is to get to the feelings behind the judgments. From that place of shared feelings, free of "right and wrong," it is possible to come together as intimate partners.

Summary Guidelines

For the Man:

1. Begin with asking yourself, "Do I want to be right or do I want my relationship?"

2. Being judgmental is toxic to a relationship. It is a self-protective avoidance of showing your own feelings.

3. Pay attention to incidents in which you say something about your partner's behavior that you dislike or want her to change. Try making another statement that states only your feelings, your inner reaction to her behavior.

4. When there is a disagreement with your partner about what happened, forget the facts, at least temporarily, so you can tune in to her feelings, and perhaps, your feelings. Often the "facts" will look different when you do that.

5. Check yourself to see if you are avoiding responsibility or behaving in some way that may be setting your partner up to acting like a judgmental authority.

6. Use "speaking for I" as a helpful technique. Make sure that you are genuinely speaking for yourself, your feelings and wants, and not making a disguised statement about your partner.

7. Be cautious about explaining your feelings. You could be indirectly justifying your reaction, thereby implying that you are in the right and your partner is in the wrong.

8. Be aware of subtle, verbal and non-verbal, judgementalness.

For the Woman:

1. Let your partner know how you react when you feel judged by him. Do it in a way that is "speaking for I."

2. After dealing with your own reaction to being judged, ask your partner to make another statement that just shows his feelings.

3. When your partner disputes your version of the facts, tell him to put aside the facts and look at the feelings, yours and his.

4. Remember that it is probably a lot more risky for your male partner to express raw feelings without rationality or justification. It may help to tell him that you understand that it is risky for him to do that.

5. Acknowledge and express appreciation for any effort that your partner makes to show his feelings behind the judgments.

5

Avoid "Forced" Power

So far we have been discussing some of the major obstacles that men face in trying to be more empathic with their partners and build healthier relationships. We've looked at how difficult it is for men to openly share their vulnerable feelings, how they struggle with the urge to rush in and "fix it," and how they cling to the need to be "right." If you are a man who has taken steps to address any of these common problems, you have made a major leap forward in the goal of tapping the power of empathy.

Now I'm going to discuss a different kind of obstacle, one that can be especially challenging for men who want to feel a sense of power in their lives and their relationships—which pretty much includes all of us. The problem relates to *how* we try to exercise power in our relationship and the *kind* of power we rely on.

In my work with couples, I have found that men express power with their partners in two very different ways. One way is to use an unhealthy *forced* power that takes the form of domination, intimidation and verbal put-downs. This comes from an inner sense of weakness and self-doubt, plus a lack of trust that your partner cares about your feelings and needs. When you are using forced power you are operating under the illusion that you can make your partner give you what you want by force and pressure.

In the other way, which is a wholesome expression of power, you simply and directly say what you feel and want. This comes from the strength of knowing that you have a right to your feelings and that your partner cares. You are confident that she will be influenced even if you don't get everything you want.

Clearly, the second form of power is the best approach for men to take in relationships, but what is best is often not what is easiest. If you are lacking in that inner strength and confidence, as many men are, you are going to be conflicted about expressing that kind of wholesome or "real" power. Unfortunately, many men find themselves struggling between two unsatisfactory options: expressing their power in a forced way or suppressing their power and becoming withdrawn.

Let's look more closely at why forced power does not work with your partner. Forced power, that is power *over* your partner so that she feels intimidated or diminished by you, is destructive. Most women experience that kind of power as a devastating blow to their self-esteem and they resent it. Even women who begin their marriage being subservient tend to give that up when they get older and more mature. If you push your authority, she may openly fight you or she may give in and behave the way you want on the surface while underneath she either makes sure that your don't really get what you want or she gets back at you in some other way.

I'll share an example of how forced power created distance in one couple's relationship. Frank and Laura would often get into a dispute that is still fairly common among couples despite the changes in gender roles in recent years. Frank would come home from a stressful day at work tired and hungry, only to find supper not ready and the children's toys scattered all over the house. He told Laura, in a way that she experienced as patronizing, how she could do a better job of disciplining the kids so they would pick up their toys and not distract her from preparing supper. On the surface, she agreed that his suggestions made sense and said she would try it. Inwardly, she didn't believe that he understood her situation, and she felt unnatural disciplining the children the way he suggested. She also resented his talking down to her.

At first Frank could see some minor changes that made it appear that his exercise of power was working. At least supper tended to be ready sooner and there was a bit less clutter of toys. But that didn't last, and things were soon back to the way they had been. Frank got more and more angry and finally ended up yelling at Laura in a threatening way. That was the beginning of a destructive, downhill pattern. Laura felt intimidated and found herself getting tense, worrying that something might make him angry. Because of her fears and self-doubts she felt unable to fight back or directly stand up to Frank. Instead, she harbored a great deal of resentment and became cold and distant from him. More and more, she met her needs for closeness and support from her relationship with her children, her friends, and her outside activities. Those were the ways she restored her self-esteem while taking the sting out of Frank's anger and disapproval. At the same time, her distance was a way for her to get back at him. Not surprisingly, Frank and Laura grew further and further apart.

Another example of a man's misguided use of power can be seen in the case of Isabelle and Sam. Isabelle asked her friend to watch their two-year-old daughter Emily while she finished an art project. Emily burned her hand on the stove when the friend left the burner on. When Sam found out about it he was furious at Isabelle and demanded that she never let her friend take care of their daughter again. Not surprisingly, Isabelle felt belittled, controlled, and judged as a bad mother. She was very resentful. Even though she also had her doubts as to whether her friend was reliable as a baby-sitter, she was not about to give in to Sam's demand. Sam's attempt to make Isabelle do what he wanted was a total failure. In the first place, he didn't get what he wanted. Isabelle felt that she had to fight being put in a one-down position, and she didn't "obey" him. Also, instead of being powerful and in control, Sam ended up feeling defeated and powerless, as well as feeling the pain of being ignored by his partner. They were both hurt and resentful. The war was on.

• **Trying to make your partner do what you want by exerting power over her is doomed to failure. Either she will openly oppose you, or she will give in and indirectly resist you. Also, she probably will look elsewhere to feel respected and restore her self-esteem.**

Both Frank and Sam were operating with the illusion that they could *make* their partner behave the way they wanted. Also, they asserted their power in a forceful, domineering way because they did not trust that their partner would be considerate of their feelings out of a sense of caring. They didn't see any other way.

Now let's imagine that Frank had felt more sure of himself and the relationship. Suppose he had a trusting attitude that recognized that both he and Laura had valid feelings and needs. He might have begun by listening to Laura describe the anxiety and pressure she was feeling in coping with their three little children while trying to cook, and acknowledge the difficult spot she was in. After fully listening to her, he could say more about *his* feelings. He could explain that he needs to relax when he comes home from a tense day at work and that it is hard for him to do that when he sees toys spread out over the living room floor. Also, he is very hungry.

In that approach, the goal is to simply understand each other without the pressure to fix the problem now. You trust in the legitimacy of your own feelings and needs and you trust that your partner is not just looking out for himself or herself. You feel safe that you are not going to be taken advantage of. Your energy and perceptions are not blocked by fighting and defending. From that place of empathic connection, the motivation and openness is there to arrive at a resolution *together*. You will be surprised at the creative ideas that emerge to improve the situation. And even if you don't get all that you want, you feel better about it because you spoke up for yourself and you are not treating your partner as if she doesn't care about you. So there are two important things to remember:

1. **Behind most couple's disputes is the question of whether your partner only cares about what he or she wants and doesn't care enough about your feelings and needs.**

2. **When there is an empathic connection there is no right and wrong and no battle. And, when couples are not blocked by fighting and defending they are much more able to come up with a solution to their problems.**

There is another realm in which an empathic connection really is the key to a successful relationship. It is that being empathic means being respectful of your partner's feelings and experience of reality. It is a way that you really care about her. It is just as important that you treat yourself as deserving empathy from *her*. That is a way that you are being respectful of yourself. Both Frank and Sam erred in assuming that they could get their partner to behave the way they wanted by force and that this was the only way to get what they wanted.

What about Sam? How could he have behaved differently when his daughter burned her hand on the stove? Imagine the difference if he had said, "That upsets me and I'm scared that if your friend baby-sits again something *worse* will happen." That would have meant giving up his illusion that he could control the situation by being demanding,. It would have meant that he might have to trust Isabelle's choices in her mothering, even if he had some degree of anxiety about that. Yet, by giving up that illusory control, or false power, he could have tapped another power—real power. He would have the power of expressing his feelings and wants, with the expectation that they will be taken seriously by his partner. And even if she didn't agree with what he wanted, he would know that he was standing up for himself in a way that was realistic and also not destructive to his partner and the relationship. That is a powerful message of strength that your partner can see. At the same time, expecting her to care about your feelings is affirming to her since it is defining her as a loving, caring person.

- **Treat your feelings and needs as valid, and expect your partner to care about them. That is a way that you are treating yourself with respect, and it tends to make you look respectful in the eyes of your partner. That is real power.**

What the Woman Can Do:

If your partner is demanding, intimidating, or belittling, you are naturally going to react with feelings such as hurt or anger. After you have dealt with your own feelings, and things have calmed down between you, let him know that you want to discuss the situation in order to make things better between you. As gently as you can, point out how his behavior has a negative effect on you and how it ultimately has a negative effect on your relationship. Tell him that you want to know and understand what bothers and upsets him. Ask him to tell you what other feelings he is having besides anger. If he has trouble identifying any other feelings, you might make some observations or guesses.

For example, Isabelle could say to Sam that she sees he is really upset about what happened to Emily, and that she is upset too. She could also try to get across to him that he doesn't have to be demanding for her to listen to him, and that she would listen just because she cares about his feelings. She might gently touch him and say something like, "We are both upset. Let's work it out together." The goal is to try to help your partner see that it is safe for him to express his more vulnerable feelings.

- **Try to be clear to your partner that pushing his power won't work, but that you care and would be responsive to his underlying emotional hurts and needs if he shares them with you.**

It is also important that you examine yourself to see if you are behaving in a way that is avoiding responsibility, which puts the load on your partner to do what is required. For example, did Isabelle give Sam the impression that she wasn't taking what happened to Emily seriously and was not being responsible about doing something about it? She might have strongly stated right from the beginning that she was upset and that *she* was questioning whether her friend could be trusted baby-sitting.

Similarly, Laura could have taken the initiative and let Frank know that she realized that he was not getting his needs met when he came home from work, and that she wanted to find a solution. That could have helped Frank to feel cared about and see that Laura was taking some responsibility in trying to find a solution to the problem. It might have relieved him of the feeling that he needed to be demanding.

- **Are you avoiding sharing responsibility in a way that may play into your partner's belief that he has to be authoritarian and demanding to get his needs met or to get something done that is best for both of you?**

Of course, men often make the same mistake of avoiding taking responsibility and then blaming their partners for being controlling. Here is an illustration that relates to Norman and Kate.

Norman sees Kate as a perfectionist who is constantly telling him what he needs to do. The problem is exacerbated by the fact that she keeps the records for his business and takes an active role in dealing with the customers. Once, Norman lost track of an order that showed the dimensions of shelves a customer wanted built. When Norman spoke with Kate on the telephone, saying he couldn't find the order, he said that he would figure out the dimensions from previous work that he had done for the customer. Kate became alarmed, worrying that he would do the job wrong. He kept trying to explain to her how he could get the dimensions figured out and do the job right. She was not convinced. After about fifteen minutes, they both gave up in frustration.

Later, when I questioned Norman, he claimed that he was confident that he would be able to get the job done correctly from records of previous work that he had done for that customer. I asked him why he argued with his wife for fifteen minutes instead of simply saying that he would handle the problem and end the discussion. He finally saw that he was trying to get Kate to agree with him. In this incident, he tried to get her stop being controlling by convincing her that he knew what he was doing. He made a feeble, ineffective attempt at exercising power, first by persuasion and then by complaining and criticizing Kate for being controlling. As long as he relied on her to change in order for him to be OK and do what he wanted to do, however, he was putting her in the position of power.

Eventually, Norman saw the truth that the only change he could count on was change in himself. Once he did that, he realized that he had to look at his own reluctance to act. He had to face the fact that, under his surface confidence, he had lots of doubt about *his own* ability to handle things. He then could see how his self-doubt came across in his interaction with Kate, and how he was contributing to her feeling that she needed to control things.

- **When your only solution to a relationship problem is that you must get the other person to change, you put yourself in a weak position. The other person has the power to change or not. Your real power comes from focusing on your own choices and facing *your* resistance to making those choices.**

When You Withdraw to Avoid Expressing Your Power

We all know that a typical problem in relationships is when men become withdrawn and emotionally inaccessible to their partners. What is not so well known is that men often put up a wall and become withdrawn because of their fear of expressing power.

Ideally, men would be able to manifest power from a base of confidence in their rights to their feelings and needs, as well as trust in their partner's caring. The truth, sadly, is that men often don't have that confidence. Without that healthy confidence, expressing power becomes a source of conflict. Rationally, you may believe in equality, but underneath you could be harboring the idea that someone must dominate, that you must dominate her or she will dominate you.

We know that boys grow up relating to each other in ways that are heavily weighted by competition, by winning and losing, and often by dominance and submission. In your relationship, while you don't want to dominate, constrict, or diminish your partner, you sure don't want her to do that to you either. It is a real challenge. As a male, you also are probably physically stronger that your female partner. You know and she knows that you could use that physical power against her. Parodoxically, that could contribute to your holding back your power since you dread the idea of physically hurting her. Also, you don't want to use physical power as a way of taking advantage of her or be accused of doing that. Women have been telling us for a long time how they have been victimized for centuries by men in a male-dominated culture. All of this can inhibit you by making you worry that if you express your will too strongly you will be one of those bad guys who does bad things to women.

Your conflict is going to be greatly intensified if you grew up in a home where you experienced one parent overpowering the other in a destructive way. Then the question of exercising power becomes a lethal issue for you, characterized by a hidden fear that someone will be crushed and someone will prevail. With that kind of background, you are faced with a serious dilemma. You don't want to repeat the pattern you grew up with, yet that is what you know. So what can you do? Unfortunately, most men either repeat their learned pattern of using power abusively or put up a wall between themselves and their partner. They attempt to avoid conflict with her by being basically uninvolved. That approach is "solving" the problem by, in effect, leaving the playing field. That's why men often vacillate between the two extremes of expressing power in a forced, abusive way, or being distant in the relationship.

Let's look at the disastrous result when men deal with their power conflict by pulling back and becoming uninvolved. Jane and Roger had a relationship that, on the surface, worked for them. Roger spent a great deal of time and energy on his career as a free-lance photographer, and Jane was a full-time homemaker who handled all the practicalities of running the house and raising their two children. While Roger occasionally expressed a preference on matters related to their home and family, he essentially left those decisions up to Jane. Eventually, it turned out that Jane was deciding more than just household matters. She made all the social and recreational decisions, such as what parties to attend, what movies or restaurants to go to, etc. Roger handled it by telling himself that he didn't care about such things.

While this set-up seemed to work in the beginning of their marriage, as time went on it became more and more obvious that there was a problem. In addition to making almost all of the decisions having to do with their lives together, Jane also was handling everything related to raising their two children. It had reached the point where Roger was hardly involved in their lives. He was spending almost all of his time on his work, and Jane became more involved in activities that did not include him. They were becoming increasingly distant from one another.

The precipitating event that brought them into therapy was a vacation. As usual, the idea for the vacation came from Jane. She wanted a family vacation at an ocean beach. Roger acquiesced, but soon after they arrived at the beach it was obvious that he was unhappy and didn't really want to be there. He made some meager attempts to cheer up and act like he was having fun, but it fell flat. The vacation was an utter failure. His usual stance of using his career as a justification for maintaining distance from his wife and family didn't hold up this time. Jane was hurt and furious. Roger felt guilty for ruining the vacation, but he had no real understanding of why or what had happened. Their problem had finally hit them like a bombshell, forcing them both to face the truth of how serious things had become.

When they came to see me, Jane expressed a lot of pain about their relationship. In the past she gave a certain amount of leeway to Roger's claim that he had to work as much as he did, but now she wasn't buying it. She saw that his distance and lack of involvement in family issues and activities was also a rejection of her and a rejection of the family. While it was hard for Roger to admit it, he knew in his gut that there was some truth in what she was saying.

- **If you continually spend an inordinate amount of time on your work, be suspicious. It is possible that your choice includes a desire to be distant from your partner.**

Not only did Jane feel rejected, she also felt that Roger had a superior and belittling attitude toward her. He showed little interest in things that concerned her and often gave the impression that he thought she didn't know what she was talking about. Recently, Roger had a significant drop in earnings. Each time Jane tried to talk with him about it he put her off, saying only that things would get better. When she did some research and made a couple of thoughtful suggestions that might increase his business, he listened halfheartedly, treating her ideas as foolish. Not surprisingly, she felt ignored and disrespected. Their financial situation reached the point where they ended up with a large debt with no visible means of recovering. Jane felt insecure and stranded. She felt as if she did not have a partner who would join with her in coping with life's problems. She began to seriously question their marriage.

Roger felt very threatened. He did not want to lose his marriage and his children. While he tried defending himself at first, his heart wasn't in it for two reasons. First, he knew that it wouldn't work for him to just put up his usual defensive arguments. He realized that he had to do something very different or risk losing it all. Also, there was a small voice inside telling him that her description of him was basically valid.

Facing the painful truth, Roger gulped and took the plunge. He admitted that there was truth in what Jane was saying about him, including the part about his superior attitude. Everything changed. Jane felt validated and seen for once, and they both felt the impact of Roger being open and vulnerable. They both recognized that Jane was being taken seriously and treated with the respect that she longed for. Also, Jane knew that it took courage for Roger to drop his guard and risk himself, which meant that he cared for her. The painful barrier between them was gone. They felt a warm connection, a closeness. It gave them a sense of hope that things could be different between them.

• **Admitting the truth in your partner's negative portrayal of you is not likely to subject you to further negativity, as men often fear. Usually your partner will appreciate it and respond positively to you. Also, you get strength and moral confidence in knowing that you are not hiding from the truth about yourself.**

Roger and Jane had survived a major crisis, though they both still had work to do in understanding themselves and their relationship. When Roger looked into his feelings he discovered that, like many men, he was afraid of his power in relation to his partner. As we explored his past, he could see why. He grew up with a tyrannical father who intimidated and belittled his mother and him. Any time his mother dared to oppose her husband he would become violently angry and emotionally abusive. Roger felt deeply troubled by how destructive this was to his mother, and he was determined that he would not treat a woman that way. For Roger to speak up for what he wanted when there was the possibility that Jane wanted something different would mean that there could be a clashing of wills. That terrified him. It was hard for him to admit it, but under his "nice guy" image, some other, not so nice feelings were lurking. He recognized that there was an inner urge to express his power the way he saw his father do it, by crushing her. And he knew he had to avoid that at all cost.

The empathic connection was the beginning of Roger and Jane's willingness to work on understanding themselves and each other. In time, with Jane's support, Roger learned that he could express his opinions and say what he wanted without being destructive like his father. And he learned that he could have influence with Jane and that he could get much of what he wanted by simply being open and direct. Each time he did that, he felt an increase in his strength and confidence, which made it easier for him to assert himself the next time. He was learning healthy power in a relationship. He felt better about himself, and he became involved with Jane and his kids in a way that was much more satisfying to him.

The example of Mark and Sally sheds further light on what happens when a man becomes emotionally withdrawn to defend against the danger of expressing hurtful power. Soon after they were married, Mark found himself being very accommodating to Sally. He seldom expressed his wants and usually went along with whatever he thought would please her. At the slightest indication that Sally was displeased with him, Mark would get upset and go into his shell. That would make Sally more upset, which would make Mark withdraw more. It created a vicious circle, ending up in their seeking therapy.

When Mark began to look at how he was excessively accommodating with Sally, he realized that this was similar to how he related to his mother. His mother was miserably unhappy in her relationship with his father, an alcoholic. Mark learned that he had unconsciously assumed the role of her savior. He was captured by a feeling that he had to make his mother's life meaningful and worthwhile. His own will and his own desires took a back seat to his mother's happiness. He tried to fight against that tendency by becoming distant from her in order to have some feeling of having his own life. Then he had another problem: a sense of guilt for rejecting her.

This pattern was now being reenacted in Mark's relationship with Sally. He felt that he had to make Sally's life his primary focus. And, when he became withdrawn to get a sense of having his own separate life, he felt guilty that he was rejecting her. The guilt made it even harder for him to assert his will. The important thing to remember:

- **When you find yourself being emotionally distant from your partner, check to see if you are holding back asserting yourself for fear of hurting your partner. Remember that real power is based on recognizing your right to express your feelings and needs.**

When You're inhibited by Guilt

Both Mark and Roger suffered from guilt that they had emotionally rejected their partners. That made them vulnerable to accusations about past mistreatment, which added to their inhibition about expressing their own feelings and wants. An example of this came up when Roger refused to say anything to Jane about something she had done that hurt him. He explained that he couldn't do that because she would point out how much more he had hurt her by his rejection and superiority. While Jane wanted Roger to express himself and be more involved with her, she also used his past behavior as a weapon, which interfered with her goal of his becoming more involved. I pointed out to Roger that while he might regret past behavior, he was changing and was not the same person. There are no debts to be repaid in relationships. In time he learned to feel less held hostage by how he was in the past and did a better job of standing up for himself.

- **While you may regret past behavior you don't need to beat yourself up. Instead, understand who you were in the past and recognize that you are no longer the same person.**

What the Woman Can Do:

If you are still angry about ways that your partner mistreated you in the past, you may need to express that anger, several times if necessary. At the same time, it is a good idea to check yourself to see if you are using the reminders of past behavior as a weapon. In that way you could be defeating yourself, since feeling blamed and guilty could cause your partner to pull away. Remember, what you really want is for your partner to be strong and caring toward you *today*.

Summary Guidelines

For the Man:

1. Exerting power over your partner so that she feels intimidated or diminished is destructive to your relationship. It is a blow to her self-esteem and she will resent it.

2. Trying to get your partner to do what you want by force is doomed to fail in several possible ways: A) She will fight you openly; B) She will comply superficially while not giving you what you really want; C) She will become emotionally distant and look for self-respect elsewhere.

3. If you are distant and avoid asserting your will, check yourself to see if you are holding back your power because of an underlying fear of hurting your partner.

4. Real power comes from two related sources: one, from confidence in your right to your feelings; and two, from trusting that you can influence your partner because she cares about your feelings and needs.

5. Treating yourself as if you expect your partner to care about your feelings is a form of self-respect. It tends to kindle your partner's respect for you.

6. Expecting your partner to genuinely care about your feelings is a positive affirmation of her as a loving person.

7. You block your power when your attention and energy is totally geared toward changing your partner's behavior. Real power comes from focusing on what you can do.

8. You can regret past behavior, but remember, if you are changing you can say, "I'm not the same person." Then you don't have to beat yourself up. Don't hold yourself hostage to your previous "sins."

9. When couples deal with a conflict by making their goal to simply understand each other, they step outside the power struggle. From that place, devoid of fighting or defensiveness, there is an opening and a freeing of energy that allows new solutions to come into awareness.

For the Woman:

1. If your partner is pushing power over you, you naturally are going to react. After you have dealt with your feelings, try to calmly explain to your partner how you are affected by his behavior, and also explain how it will ultimately have a bad effect on your relationship.

2. Encourage him to express the hurts and fears that are behind his demands, intimidation, or put-downs. Let him know that you care about his feelings and will be influenced if he risks showing those feelings to you.

3. Check yourself to see if you are avoiding taking responsibility in your actions, which may play into your partner's feeling that he must run things in a dominating way.

4. While it is important to allow and express your anger about your partner's past behavior, don't use it as a weapon. That will

have a negative effect on your relationship. You don't want your man to feel he has a debt that can never be repaid, which can leave him fearing that you won't love him.

6

Learn to Express "Clean" Anger

Let's explore another truth that most men fail to recognize or understand, a truth that is very much related to power. This truth relates to anger. Men, contrary to what you may have been taught or have always believed, anger is not necessarily good or bad, constructive or destructive. It is how you relate to anger, how and why you express it or avoid expressing it, and how it is received that makes it positive or negative.

While it is not always necessary or desirable to express anger, it is important that you have the *genuine option* to express it or not. And if you suppress your anger it's important to know the real reason for suppressing it. Typically, men say it's because, "It won't accomplish anything" or "It will hurt her feelings" or "It will make things worse." They sometimes explain holding back their anger on moral or religious grounds. Often that is a deception, and the real reason is some inner fear or inhibition. Whatever your reason, it is important that you try to be honest with yourself as to why you hold back your anger.

Physical attack and character assassination are obviously destructive. In the previous chapter I pointed out how anger linked to the kind of power that intimidates or belittles your partner can severely damage your relationship. When Frank shouted at Laura in a threatening way for not having the children's toys picked up and supper ready, he was being abusive. It led to a toxic downturn in their relationship. When Sam angrily demanded that Isabelle stop using her friend as a baby-sitter, he was also being destructive. Isabelle felt disrespected and fought back. Sam ended up feeling ignored and powerless. In both cases, anger *in itself* was not the problem. The problem was that the anger was tied to intimidation, power, and control.

Both of these men could have expressed their anger more constructively. For example, Frank could have simply said that he was angry. While he may have used an angry tone, he could at least have said it without shouting. Even if Laura felt a moment of anxiety it would have been much less frightening and denigrating than what she felt when he yelled at her. And Sam could have shown his anger at Isabelle for relying on her friend to baby-sit without expressing it as a demand. She would have been much less likely to feel insulted as if she were being treated like a disobedient child. When your anger is not tied to intimidation, when it is not belittling, controlling, or rejecting, that is "clean" anger. Clean anger is much easier for your partner to deal with, making it much more likely that she can handle it without reacting defensively.

You may believe that even clean, straightforward anger will have a negative effect on your partner. She may take it as criticism or intimidation no matter how you express it. Then you need to decide, on balance, what is the best choice, bearing in mind that your partner and your relationship could be damaged if not expressing your anger results in your becoming more distant. At the same time, it is important to remember that if she has a lot of trouble emotionally handling non-excessive, clean anger, that is *her* issue and her responsibility to work on in herself. It's important that you keep in mind that your purpose is not to hurt her but to express your feelings, and that you want to be honest and present with your partner. Also, try to remember that your behavior is not just looking out for yourself but is also based on an understanding that honesty and openness are what is best for the relationship. That perspective frees you from the trap of guilt that comes from feeling that you have been unnecessarily hurtful to her.

- **When you express anger, do it in a way that is not frightening or disrespectful. While clean anger may result in a temporary rift, it is not likely to be damaging to your relationship. Remember, the goal is to be honest, to express yourself and to help build positive contact with your partner.**

If you are like most men, you probably feel the need to be rational, which means you are not allowed to be angry unless it's justified. So when you suspect that your anger is not justified, you may find yourself pushing it down and trying to ignore it, or worse, you don't even let yourself feel it. As a result, you are emotionally constricted in a way that blocks your energy and aliveness. Also, if you do express your anger you may suffer from guilt and/or self-criticism. Another problem occurs when you try to prove that your anger is justified. When you do that, you are making yourself right and your partner wrong, which we discussed in an earlier chapter. Then it is no longer just clean anger. You are being judgmental. You are telling her that she behaved wrongly or badly in some way.

There is a thin line between being told that you behaved badly and getting the message that you *are* bad, or that something is wrong with you. What if Sam, to bolster his case, had tacked on a list of reasons that Isabelle should not have trusted her friend to baby-sit? Suppose he tied his anger to critical comments like the fact that she knew her friend was flaky and not reliable, or that she cared more about going off and doing her art work than the safety of her child? Those kinds of statements are more than just anger. They are hurtful, critical remarks that are likely to make her feel unacceptable and unloved. And she is almost sure to react in a defensive way, which could make matters worse.

The important lesson that both men *and* women need to learn in relationships is that anger, and all their feelings, are valid in themselves. They have nothing to do with rationality. If you are angry, you are angry. You don't have to be right or justified. When you don't claim that you are necessarily justified in your feelings, you can be angry without being judgmental toward your partner or yourself. Not only does it make your anger much more tolerable to your partner, it also has the benefit of making you freer to experience and express your feelings.

- **Your feelings are valid and don't need to be rational or justified. Not having to be rational or right frees you and your partner from the endless "right and wrong" battle and enables you to be less constricted and more alive.**

Being on the Receiving End of Anger

While you can experience your partner's expression of anger as a threatening attack, usually the major source of suffering is the meaning we ascribe to it: "She hates me." "He is contemptuous of me." "He wants nothing to do with me." "I do bad things to her." "I am totally inept." "I am a failure as a partner." "Our relationship is going to end." These are the kinds of thoughts in the background, perhaps only vaguely recognized, that can cause lots of pain.

If you are very upset by your partner's anger, try to determine if your partner is attaching anger to power, control, or being judgmental. If you are convinced that your partner is doing that, say that it is not okay with you. Tell your partner that you can accept the anger but you don't want to be controlled, put down, or intimidated—whichever applies. If you realize or suspect that your partner is primarily just expressing anger without those other attachments, then consider that your upsetness may be an over-reaction. Do you have a special difficulty dealing with anger no matter how it is expressed? If you do, it is a good idea to let your partner know that you recognize your problem and, also, that you take responsibility to work on dealing with this issue in yourself.

- **If you suspect that you are over-reacting to your partner's anger, be open about the meaning you tend to give to that anger. Take responsibility to face and work on your own sensitivity.**

Fearing a Loss of Control

A common reason men hold back anger with their partner is fear of their aggressive impulses. Boys in our society learn physical expression of aggression at an early age. Winning and physically fighting back if attacked is part of our evolutionary heritage. When a man gets in touch with strong anger he may sense an urge to physically attack the person he is angry at. This tendency is there with women as well, but usually to a lesser degree. If that aggressive feeling gets stirred up with your partner, it can be scary. You may be afraid that if you let yourself feel the full force of your anger, you would physically hurt your partner. For the vast majority of men, there is a thread of control that would enable them to hold back physical violence. However, if you are one of those men who actually loses control, you need to take concrete preventive steps such as leaving the scene until you calm down. Getting professional help also can enable you to learn other ways to appropriately deal with your anger.

What if you know that your anger is linked to the urge to overpower your partner? You don't want to intimidate or denigrate her, but you recognize that you have the tendency to do that when you're angry. You not only want to avoid being emotionally destructive to your partner, but you also don't want to face the consequences of how she will react to you. So instead of expressing your anger you hold it back or bury it. Now you have another problem. Typically, when men push down anger they become emotionally withdrawn or put up a wall between themselves and their partner, which can seriously damage their relationship.

- **If holding back your anger means becoming emotionally withdrawn, that could be more destructive to the relationship than the anger, even if your anger may be expressed unskillfully.**

Men are often puzzled by behavior that they later discover is the result of anger that they were not aware of. Remember Charlie and Michelle? Charlie couldn't understand what Michelle was upset about regarding his behavior at that party. It took some time before he was able to face the truth that he had been flirtatious with other women, and that it was partly a way that he was getting back at Michelle for rejecting him sexually. He acted out his anger instead of expressing it directly.

A young man I recently saw couldn't understand why his girlfriend was deeply embarrassed by something he "innocently" said to a friend. Later, he realized that he had been harboring hurt feelings toward his girlfriend for ignoring him. That awareness enabled him to see that what he had said to his friend was not just an innocent remark. It was a hidden way of wounding her. As long as he was not in touch with his anger he couldn't see that he had done anything hurtful.

We can see a more serious case of buried anger in the example of Jane and Roger. Roger was so afraid of being crushingly tyrannical like his father that he felt he had to avoid all possible conflict with Jane. To do that, he left almost all family decisions up to her. The result was that he became more and more isolated from her and the children, with devastating consequences. Roger failed to see the problems as they were developing. His distance may *appear* to serve two purposes. First, he avoided the danger of becoming angry in an abusive way. Second, his anger was being expressed indirectly by his withholding closeness from Jane and by manifesting a superior attitude toward her. Ultimately, however, neither Roger nor his relationship benefited at all.

- **Holding back anger can be harmful not only when it creates distance in your relationship, but also because that anger will probably come out indirectly.**

Whether you express or withhold anger, it is important that you are *aware* of the feeling when it is there. When you know that you are angry you can choose if and when to express it. Awareness, which we will discuss in more detail in the next chapter, gives you choices. And, whichever choice you make, try to be aware of the cost of expressing your anger and the cost of withholding it.

Constructive Expression of Anger

A good example of a couple dealing positively with both mild and intense anger occurred in the case of Linda and Robert. It began with their discussion of an upcoming Board of Supervisors meeting in which decisions would be made that would have an important impact in their community. The plan was for Robert to attend the meeting, since Linda was unable to go. The discussion ended with Linda saying in an irritable tone of voice, "When you go to the meeting be awake and be aware!" While they both knew that Robert would often tune out in social situations, he felt stung by Linda's comment. He looked her in the eye and said, "You're cutting me down. That pisses me off."

Instead of becoming defensive, Linda admitted that her comment was a put-down, with the clear implication that Roger tuning out at this meeting was definitely not okay with her. After her admission, the atmosphere completely changed. The anger and hurt were virtually gone, and they were able to be light with each other. She was able to tease him about his tendency to tune out in a way that he felt accepted rather than maligned. What began as a destructive exchange ended up with warmth and affection.

Robert was pleased that he dealt with the incident in a much better way than he would have in the past. Typically, he would have reacted by withdrawing and licking his wounds, which could last for days. There were also times that he had exploded with rage that was verbally and even physically threatening. His outburst would trigger a serious disruption in the relationship, and Robert ended up feeling weak and very self-critical.

What enabled Robert to behave differently this time? For one thing, it helped that this was familiar territory. He and Linda had previously talked openly about his tendency to not pay attention in certain situations. The fact that Robert admitted this tendency, even though he was somewhat ashamed of it, took some of the edge off of Linda's anger. Her anger was also lessened by the fact that he did not question or deny her right to be annoyed by his tuning out behavior. He had become more tolerant of this fact about himself since it was out in the open, and he knew that his partner still accepted and loved him even with this behavior that was sometimes irritating to her.

Another reason Robert handled this situation better was that, through self-exploration, he had learned to be less afraid of his anger. Instead of being stuck in the impossible trap of having only two choices, to either explode with intense anger or shut down, he was now able to express more moderate forms of anger such as annoyance or resentment.

- **If you find that you vacillate between expressing anger in an explosive, aggressive way or shutting down, you are stuck in a lose-lose trap. You need to get to the middle ground of being capable of expressing anger moderately.**

When they went to bed that night, Robert was feeling encouraged by his own progress and feeling very good about their relationship. They said good night with a warm embrace. In the middle of the night, however, he woke up in the shock of feeling very angry toward Linda. After he and Linda had arrived at such a loving place with each other, this was not a welcome experience. Robert did not want to believe that he was that sensitive and could still react so strongly to something Linda said, but there was a clear gap between what he wanted to believe about himself and the truth. As he lay there feeling distressed, wishing his anger would go away, he found that the opposite was happening. His anger grew stronger. While he suspected that he was over-reacting, he chose to stay with the feeling, to face the truth of what he actually felt instead of focusing on what he wanted to feel or thought he should feel.

Robert's choice paid off. By not fighting his feelings he found that he could be clearer, and he soon realized that he was reacting not only to having felt put down by Linda but to something else. He saw that there was a deeper issue of feeling that he was being bossed by Linda, that she was treating him like he was a child. He felt disrespected, and that's why he was so hot with anger. He was tempted to wake Linda up and blurt out his feelings, but he knew that would probably lead to a destructive fight. He also considered getting up and having a drink or two, but he knew that this would only be a temporary escape and would blunt the clarity that he needed to deal with the problem. Instead, he just let himself feel his anger and made a decision that he would express it in the morning. He found that this decision released him from obsessive thinking and enabled him to go back to sleep.

In the morning, Robert did openly tell Linda what he was furious about. He made no claims to himself or to Linda that his feelings were reasonable, healthy, or justified. Since he did not feel the need to be justified, he did not have to point to Linda as the one at fault. Linda said nothing and just listened empathically while he laid out his feelings. There was no focus on right or wrong and no defensiveness. Robert had the common experience of finding that when he felt listened to in an accepting way, his anger quickly subsided.

When he was finished, Linda expressed *her* anger toward him for his condescending attitude toward her and things that she cared about, including the Board of Supervisors' meeting. Since he felt that Linda had listened to his feelings respectfully in a validating way, he was able and willing listen to her when she spoke for her feelings. They both had the experience of expressing and being sincerely listened to without defensiveness. They felt an empathic connection. They ended up feeling trusting, open, and loving toward each other. Remember, recognizing the validity of your partner's *feelings* is what counts. It does not necessarily mean that you agree with your partner's conclusions.

- **If you listen empathically, which means you understand and respect the validity of your partner's feelings, it is much easier for your partner to listen empathically to *your* feelings.**

The option to express clean anger is also important from the point of view of self-esteem. When Robert did not put up with Linda's belittling and bossiness, and yet didn't react with impotent rage, he was making a healthy declaration of self-esteem. In essence, he was saying, "*I don't deserve to be treated that way.*" His anger was an important and valuable part of his ability to stand up for himself. Even when anger is expressed in an unskillful or destructive way it is important to recognize the part that is an expression of self-esteem.

- **Whether the anger is yours or your partner's, make sure that you honor that aspect of the anger that is an attempt to affirm self worth.**

Getting to Feelings under Your Anger

Sometimes just expressing your anger is all you need to do. Your partner may grasp what's behind your anger without your having to spell it out. Often, however, to make a real connection with your partner you have to let her know what you are angry about. It's not enough to say what your partner did that made you angry. You need to be aware of and at some point willing to share the feelings like hurt, humiliation, fear, or a sense of inadequacy that are the source of your anger. It is those underlying vulnerable feelings that are not accessed and not expressed by men that often prevent real communication. A major reason that Robert and Linda were able to come together was that they both knew a lot about each other's sensitivities from previous discussions. Linda knew that Robert was sensitive to feeling cut down or bossed by her. Robert knew that Linda was sensitive to feeling ignored or not taken seriously by him.

As important as it is to learn to express your anger and do it cleanly, it is also helpful to keep in mind that it is not always necessary to express anger at all. Why? Sometimes it is sufficient and, at times, preferable to just share your underlying feelings. There are times when you may need to begin with anger in order to open the door to your other feelings. There are other times when you can just go directly to the underlying feelings. The point is to be honest as to whether your not expressing anger is a defensive avoidance or if you genuinely don't need to. Telling your partner "That hurts me" or "I feel cut down" may be all that you need to say. It does not mean that you are whining or complaining or being a wimp. It can be said in a strong, straightforward way. It just means that you are admitting the truth, which usually takes courage. And that is something you can feel good about. Of course your woman knows that she has the power to do and say things that hurt you. Admitting that is facing reality.

If anger leads to a disruption in your relationship, it is a good idea to come back, perhaps after a break with time to calm down, and *try again*. You don't have to get it right the first time. Hopefully, you are able to be less defensive on your second try.

• **Whether or not you begin with anger, ultimately, communicating and accepting each other's vulnerable feelings and sensitivities is the basis for an empathic connection that strengthens your relationship.**

Other Factors in Reconciliation

Robert and Linda were able to come together in a warm, loving way after both confrontations. Much of their success came from their ability and willingness to openly share their areas of sensitivity and to listen to each other empathically. Also, after the first confrontation, they made good use of humor through gentle teasing. The element of *lightness* that humor brings to a situation can make anger much more tolerable. It can be useful after an angry exchange or it may serve to take the sting out of the anger right from the start. Of course, humor only works when the anger is not too intense or the intensity has subsided. Be careful that your teasing is not laced with a hostile edge. It's better to skip the teasing if that is the case.

While it is important to do everything we can to reach an empathic understanding with our partners after an angry exchange, it is not always possible, or at least not possible at that particular time. In that case, peacemaking gestures may provide at least some form of coming together. Just letting your partner know that you feel badly about what happened or that you are unhappy about the distance between you can help to begin reconnecting. A friendly offering or a gentle touch can sometimes be powerful magic. We are told not to act like an animal, but recent animal studies have shown that peacemaking may actually be as biologically natural as aggression. Some primates tend to reunite after having a fight, often with affectionate behavior such as kissing and embracing.

- **If you are not able to empathically break through a disruption, try a peacemaking gesture. Bear in mind that there is an unresolved issue that may need to be dealt with at a later time.**

Summary Guidelines

1. While it is not always necessary or desirable to express anger, it is important that you be aware of the feeling and that you know the real reasons for holding it back if that is your choice. What matters is that you have a genuine option to express it or not.

2. Physical attack or character assassination are abusive and destructive and absolutely should be avoided. If you have difficulty controlling those behaviors, try taking time out and leaving the scene until you calm down.

3. Strive to express your anger in a way that is just "clean" anger, not tied to being intimidating, judgmental, or controlling.

4. Even if you suspect that your anger is irrational or unfair, don't let that stop you. You may need to tell your partner that you are not claiming that your anger is rational.

5. Try to be aware of how you tend to interpret your partner's anger, like what you imagine she is feeling toward you under the anger. Share that with your partner. If you see that you are

over-reacting, take responsibility to face and work on your sensitive issue.

6. Remember, if holding back your anger causes you to be withdrawn, that may be more destructive to your relationship than expressing it even if your expression is not clean and skillful.

7. Look at things that you do that bother your partner. Check yourself to see if you may be holding back anger that is coming out indirectly. See if you are willing to express your anger directly.

8. Check to see if you are pushing down anger out of fear of your impulses. Remember, feelings are not actions. Having violent images doesn't mean that you need to or will act on them.

9. If you are stuck in the dysfunctional polarity of either explosive anger or shutting down, you need to get to the middle ground of being able to express mild and moderate anger.

10. Remember to honor, in yourself and in your partner, that aspect of anger that is standing up for yourself as an affirmation of self-esteem.

11. Check to see if you are sharing the feelings behind the anger. Are you willing to let your partner know your vulnerable feelings such as hurt, humiliation, or a sense of inadequacy? If you are reluctant, what is your reluctance?

12. When there is a disruption in your relationship, try starting again, even if it is just telling your partner that you are upset by the rift between you. See if you can learn more about your partner's vulnerable feelings while exposing more of your own.

13. Try using humor in dealing with annoyances. Playful teasing can be helpful when it is delivered in an affectionate, friendly way and is received as such.

14. If you can't break through a disruption, try peacemaking, and work on the unresolved issue at a later time if necessary.

7

Awareness: Know What You Feel

Awareness, especially knowing what we feel and what we want, is fundamental for all of us in living full, vital, and authentic lives. Yet we often confuse what we actually feel with what we want to feel or think we should feel. To be aware means being willing to experience all kinds of feelings, including those we may consider irrational or unwarranted. It means allowing feelings that may be painful, frightening, or shameful. It is seeing ourselves as we actually are rather than according to our self-image.

If you face the truth of what you feel or want, you may hurt or displease someone you care about. That could lead to a serious conflict with the person that matters most to you. While this is a challenging issue for all of us, it is a special problem in relationships for men because, as we have discussed, they generally tend to be less in touch with their feelings than women.

Back in Chapter 2, we explored how learning to become comfortable with vulnerable feelings can help men enhance their intimate connections with their partner. But there's a difference between being comfortable with your feelings and being fully aware of what they are. In order to empathize with your partner you have to be able to call up within yourself a feeling that is comparable to what your partner is feeling. If you are defended against those feelings you can't get a real sense of what she is actually experiencing. You may think you are being empathic but you're not.

This is often confusing. Even when you may be able to verbally describe your partner's feeling, you see that she is not satisfied. She still doesn't feel understood. The problem is that your understanding may be correct on the surface, but you are not with her at the same level of intensity. It's like knowing that your partner is upset and it bothers you, but you're not much affected by it. Then, when she feels not understood despite your sincere effort to be empathic, you may wind up feeling threatened and despairing. You could see yourself as a disappointment, a failure, maybe even unlovable to her.

In many of the examples of couples we have looked at so far, serious disruptions occurred when the men were defensive and lacked awareness. They were not in touch with their feelings and they didn't understand their behavior that was tied to those feelings.

When Michelle confronted Charlie about his ignoring her at the previous night's party, his knee-jerk reaction was defensiveness. He vigorously denied it and came up with a rational argument, giving "objective" evidence that he had not ignored her. He felt threatened by Michelle's anger and disapproval and he had a large stake in believing that he wouldn't behave that way since he was a "good guy and considerate husband." At the same time, he couldn't see that what Michelle was saying could be correct since he had no understanding of his behavior and the emotions that were driving it. His behavior at the party, as well as his reaction to Michelle's confrontation, was the product of both defensiveness and lack of self-awareness.

The way that Charlie finally salvaged the situation was to put aside the whole question of the facts, and who is right or wrong, so he could just listen to her subjective reality. It was a risk for him to do that. Once you put aside your viewpoint to listen to the other person's subjective reality you become vulnerable to the possibility that they are also objectively correct. As it turned out, when Charlie looked at himself more honestly, he could see that he had actually been flirtatious with other women and had not spent much time with Michelle. Once he took that step, his awareness opened up. He began to recognize some of the feelings that were behind his actions. He realized that he had been harboring feelings of hurt and anger toward Michelle for rejecting him sexually. From there he was able to take the next step and see that his flirting with other women was a way of boosting his wounded ego and getting back at her at the same time.

Awareness from the start could have helped Charlie to avoid the disruption in his relationship in two ways. He could have sensed that there was some truth in what Michelle was saying, and his behavior could have shown her that he was seriously considering her view of what happened. Also, the entire situation could have been avoided from the beginning if he had faced and openly expressed his hurt and angry feelings about her sexual rejection. Then the feelings would not have been coming out indirectly in the form of unconscious acting out behavior. It's also possible that Michelle and Charlie could have talked about his feelings of rejection and worked it out. But even if they didn't successfully work it out he would have felt strength in knowing that he was not holding back or hiding his feelings, but was expressing them openly and directly.

• **When you lack awareness, especially when you don't know your feelings, your behavior is driven by forces out of your control. When you are aware of your feelings and are free to express them openly, you become stronger. You are standing up for your right to be who you are.**

With awareness, you have choices in your behavior and choices in how you respond to your partner. Sometimes you may choose to defend yourself when she challenges you, while other times you may decide to risk revealing vulnerable feelings. You are in charge. This is important in all aspects of your life, but in your relationship with your partner it is crucial.

All of us have ways in which we act self-protective and avoid facing the truth about ourselves. I'll name some of the common beliefs that block awareness. Most of these beliefs are a special problem for men. As you will notice, we have touched upon many of these beliefs in our earlier discussions, but I've grouped them together here so we can see the full picture of what gets in the way of awareness. After covering these common beliefs, I will present some simple exercises that can help men *and* women cultivate a greater awareness of what they feel.

1. "Be a man." "Big boys don't cry." Males learn from an early age to push back vulnerable feelings such as hurt, fear, neediness, and shame, which they are likely to consider signs of weakness.

We know that boys and girls are socialized differently in how to deal with feelings. If a girl is feeling hurt, sad, or inadequate, she can be open about those feelings. Her friends are not going to ostracize her or put her down. It's totally different with boys. If a boy is feeling slighted by a friend, or if he is not chosen to be on a team, or if he is too frightened to do something his friends are doing, he is going to do everything possible to *not* show his feelings. He can't let himself show that he is hurt, scared, or feeling inadequate. That would mean that he is weak and the other boys will ridicule and reject him. Also, if he is seen as weak he may be in danger of being bullied and beat up. The saddest part is that the boy himself feels that he is weak for having vulnerable feelings, which, of course, is carried over into manhood. The effect, which we first explored in Chapter 2, is that lots of men trying to obey the relentless inner voice saying "Be a man" bury their vulnerable feelings so that they are ignored or discarded. Sadly, what often happens is that their protective wall blocks their ability to experience and recognize not only feelings such as hurt, shame, and fear but feelings in general, including *positive* feelings such as tenderness, appreciation, affection, and love. As a result, men suffer and their partners suffer.

2. Feelings need to be rational. Usually this means that feelings not only need to make sense but also must be justified and fair.

Women, not just men, have difficulty with this, but it is often more of a problem for men since they are more inclined to put a high value on rationality. When you focus on rationality you are in your head, not in your body where your feelings are. Feelings are feelings; they are not necessarily reasonable or fair. And if you must be rational, you can't let yourself recognize many of your feelings. If you do recognize "irrational" feelings you must ignore them or try to overcome them. And, of course, your partner's feelings that you consider irrational become invalid. You focus on the objective "facts" and ignore her subjective reality. As we've seen in earlier examples, this can easily lead to a fruitless argument of who's right and who's wrong. Besides, even if you are right about the facts, her feelings are valid. Invalidating her feelings is bad enough, but if she feels that you are criticizing her for being irrational that's even more destructive. You may need to ask yourself the question: "Do I want to be right or do I want my relationship?"

3. If I feel something I'll have to act on it.

This fear is a special problem for men since they tend to be more action oriented. If a man is feeling upset or unhappy with his partner, he may have fantasies of leaving and being with someone else. While these imaginings could be comforting in one way, they could also be threatening to him if he has a sense that he must act upon them.

Anger toward his partner may be especially disturbing because men have a tendency to connect anger with physical violence. As noted earlier, one of a man's common fears is that if he allows his full expression of anger he will do bodily harm to his woman and she, being physically weaker, will not be able to stop him.

4. Feelings, and thoughts tied to those feelings, have a solid, literal, and even permanent existence.

Men are more likely than women to look upon feelings in this way. Women typically have a more fluid, less attached attitude toward feelings, seeing them as experiences that come and go. In an outburst of anger she may accuse him of being self-righteous, inconsiderate, uncaring, etc. Instead of simply receiving those statements as her current feelings tied to something specific that just happened, he might believe that this is her general conclusion about him. So he feels not only attacked or criticized but also condemned as an unacceptable partner, which would be devastating. So he may react by becoming enraged or withdrawn and despairing. If he had more understanding that she is primarily expressing her feelings of the moment rather than meaning it as a "cast in stone" view of him, he would be less disturbed and less likely to behave in an extreme way. She could feel hurt and discouraged since she may be looking for an empathic response to what is bothering her, not realizing that he is feeling too devastated to be empathic.

Also, because of his tendency to think of feelings as solid and permanent, he could worry that *his* negative feelings toward his partner mean that there is something seriously wrong with the relationship. In response, he may deny or push those feelings out of his awareness, which would cause him to put up a defensive wall of falseness and create distance between them.

5. Painful feelings are a problem to be fixed rather than experienced and understood.

No one likes pain, and there is a natural pull in all of us to eliminate or reduce painful feelings when they occur. Men, generally being problem-solvers, tend to jump to a solution, looking to get rid of the painful feeling. If his partner points out a problem that affects them both, he may turn to that fix-it response we explored earlier or just deny that there is a problem. If he feels she is putting the responsibility on him or criticizing him, he could react by attacking her or by trying to prove she is wrong instead of facing that what she is saying may be true. He is reacting instead of first taking a moment to just experience the painful feeling. If he were able to become aware of the feeling and experience it, his action would be more effective because it would be coming from a place of understanding and control.

6. If I allow myself to fully experience a negative feeling it will overpower me and I will be out of control.

This is a common fear in both men and women. Sometimes I suggest to clients that they go more deeply into experiencing their feelings of sadness, despair, or neediness, or other feelings they consider undesirable, such as jealousy, pride, or greed. They often resist my suggestion initially, and when I probe, I find that they are afraid either that if they go more deeply into the feeling they will feel worse about themselves or that the feeling will get more powerful and take them over. Actually, with the possible exception of someone who has a severe mental illness, the opposite is the case. The truth is that when you push a feeling down, out of awareness, it actually has greater power, and is affecting you no matter how much you resist it. Usually, when you allow yourself to fully experience the feeling that you're resisting, bringing it out into the light of day, it may seem stronger at first, then it lessens in intensity and loses its grip over you. You are more in control and you have more energy because you are not at war with yourself, fighting your feeling.

It is true that there are times when a confrontation between partners in a relationship will bring up a flood of feelings that are so intense that they seem unbearable to either of you. This is something that happens to men more than women, and it often occurs when the man feels criticized by his partner. He may react with an explosive rage or by stonewalling, refusing to communicate in a desperate attempt to protect himself. The most effective strategy is to have an agreement that, if there is a sign that one of you is feeling overwhelmed, you take a break and come back to your discussion later.

7. If I admit to feelings like fear, shame, and self-doubt, my partner will disrespect me.

As we saw in Chapter 2, this is primarily a male distortion. "She will think I am a wimp, not a man." Because men usually believe that having those feelings is a sign of weakness, it is not surprising that they would assume that their women partners have the same belief. The truth is that while some women who struggle with dependency problems may need to view their partners as an invincible rock, most women know better. They know that these are human feelings shared by everyone. Ironically, if the man denies such feelings, she is likely to see that as his need to hide from the truth about himself and view *that* as a sign of weakness. In fact, she is more likely to think more highly of him for being honest and courageous in owning up to those feelings. Not only that, but she probably would see his self-disclosure as a wonderful sign that he is willing to risk himself in order to be close to her. This could be valuable to her in other ways. It gives her the chance to express the nurturing aspect of herself. Also, it could make it easier for her to show her "weakness" without worrying that she is in an inferior position in the relationship.

8. If I admit that she has the ability to hurt, humiliate, and threaten me, she will take advantage of that in order to dominate or control me.

Again, this belief plays into the man's fear that he is weak, not a man. To protect himself he may try to assert his power in some way, possibly becoming hurtful, threatening, or domineering. Or he may react by becoming withdrawn. Both would be destructive to the relationship. Women know that they can cause their partners to feel hurt or threatened. It's no secret and doesn't make him more susceptible to being dominated or controlled. Second, if she didn't feel that she could cause those kind of feelings in her man she would doubt how much he is involved in the relationship. While dominance and control may be present to some degree in all relationships, it is important to recognize this simple fact:

• **Most women are much more interested in closeness than dominance.**

9. If my partner knew about my negative feelings toward her, she would be deeply hurt.

You don't want to hurt your partner for lots of reasons. You care about her, you want to be considerate, you don't want to think of yourself as a critical, hurtful person, you see yourself as your woman's protector, etc. It is true that if you tell her you don't like some of the ways she acts, she may be hurt or angry at first. Yet men tend to make two mistakes in this area. One, they underestimate their partner's ability to detect the negative feelings he is harboring. Men are often surprised to find that the woman knew he was having these feelings all the time. The second mistake is in underestimating the harmful effect of burying or holding back negative feelings. Defending against those feelings often results in emotional withdrawal and possibly inner resentment, which comes out in indirect, unconscious ways. This happened when Charlie indulged in flirtatious acting out at a party instead of telling Michelle what he was feeling. Another example was Roger's holding back his resentment of Jane's controlling behavior, which led to his complete pulling back from family involvement. In both cases there was a serious disruption in the relationship.

Generally, women are much more hurt by the man's defensive distance than they would be if he expressed his negative feelings directly to her.

10. If I show my deepest, hidden feelings, no one, including my partner, will be empathic, so it's best to forget about those feelings.

This is a fear that all of us are subject to. What if I reveal feelings that I am ashamed or critical of? What if I share my deepest fears and secret longings? Will anyone, including my partner, respond not only with tolerance but understanding and care? Men are especially likely to keep a certain distance from their partners because of this fear. Because a man usually is more open with his woman partner than anyone else, it often means going through his whole life with the loneliness of not having really shared himself. The idea that men don't need that kind of closeness is wrong. Men need to be known and understood as much as women do, despite their defensive walls. When a man does risk revealing his "secret feelings" he usually finds that his partner is much more accepting and empathic than he expects. Beyond that, he finds that she appreciates his willingness to risk himself, to be deeply involved with her for the sake of intimacy and love.

How She Reacts to These Blocks

As a woman, when you see your partner operating under these kinds of false beliefs, it is important to respond supportively. As we've seen before, your responses to him can help or hinder his attempts at becoming more aware of his feelings and becoming more willing to share them with you.

First, avoid statements such as "Act like a man" or criticisms that imply that he doesn't measure up as a man. That would play into some of his worse fears and contribute to his defensiveness. It could also contribute to a general feeling of self-doubt, which would make it harder for him to behave in a decisive, responsible way. That would be weakening to him, a loss to you, and the relationship would suffer.

It is important for you to check your own beliefs and feelings to see if you are buying into the myth that real men are free of feelings such as hurt, shame, and self-doubt. Also, try to be aware if you have strong dependency needs, needs that are so strong that you resist allowing him to have any weaknesses. These could be ways that you increase his defensive behavior and sabotage your desire to have a partner that is open and emotionally intimate with you. It would help if, by both your words and actions, you show him that you do not consider him weak or unmanly for having vulnerable feelings, and that you appreciate and respect him for taking the risk of disclosing those feelings. That appreciation and respect could also serve as evidence that you are mainly interested in connecting with him, rather than dominating or controlling him.

Women sometimes make the mistake of getting over-involved in a rational argument when the man focuses on "the facts." Let him know that you want him to be aware of your reality, your feelings, even if he disagrees about what happened, and that you are willing to listen to his feelings as well. After that, you both may choose to state your different versions of what happened, with the understanding that you will try to avoid the fruitless argument of who's right and who's wrong.

Try to refrain from making absolute statements about him and/ or your relationship that are mostly coming out of the heat of the moment. Unless you mean it as a well thought out conclusion, avoid saying things like, "you're selfish," "you're inconsiderate," "you don't care about me," "we don't get along." He may think that you are ready to give up on the relationship and react accordingly. Sometimes it is a good idea to spell out that you are not condemning him or giving up on the relationship, but rather that you want to change things.

When your partner comes up with a denial or a quick solution to a problem that affects you both, tell him that you are not expecting him to have an instant solution. Let him know that you want to connect with him and feel that you are not alone in your concerns. At the same time, it is a good idea to check yourself to see if you may be giving him a message, overt or subtle, that it is his responsibility to fix such problems, which could be defeating your goal of sharing feelings.

When your partner is being distant or showing other signs of holding something back, consider that he may have some negative feelings toward you that he is reluctant to express. Again, it is wise to look into yourself to see if you have put out the message that you can't tolerate his anger, disapproval, etc. It would be helpful if you let him know that you are strong enough to handle his negative feelings toward you, that you are not going to fall apart and, further, that his expressing these feelings is much easier for you to take than his emotional distance.

Exercises in Awareness

1. <u>Awareness Continuum:</u> This exercise is analogous to doing finger exercises when you are learning to play the piano. It's a process in

which you follow and state everything you notice: body sensations, your movement, sounds, sights, thinking, feelings, etc. At first you start each statement with the words "Now I'm aware..." Then you speed up the process and skip the phrase "now I'm aware" when it slows you up. For example, you might say, "I'm aware my hands are folded. Now I'm aware of tension in my stomach. I'm aware of laughing. Breathing, hearing the bird, looking at you, wondering what you're thinking, looking at the picture, moving my head, licking my lips, pausing, breathing..." Try to get to a speed where it seems that there is almost no space between your reported awareness. If you pause, say "aware of pausing" or just "pausing." You can never go as fast as your actual perception, but you can get better and better at it. It may be helpful to experiment doing this with a partner. If you are doing it alone, it is best in the beginning to speak out loud. Later, you may be able to do it silently when you are around other people.

It is not necessary to do the exercise for a long time. I have done it for as little as ten seconds and discovered something I was not conscious of. It could be a simple thing, such as noticing that I am tensing my neck, or it could be something deeper, such as noticing that I'm angry or feeling hurt. The more you do the exercise, the more you benefit. You not only are able to make discoveries at the time you are doing the exercise, but it also helps you to develop the habit of tuning in to yourself.

2. <u>Inner Dialogue or Empty Chair Technique:</u> In this exercise, you picture your partner, or someone you are having a problem with, sitting in a chair directly facing you. You try to get a sense of actually seeing them and looking them in the eye. Then you say what you feel like saying to them. It's not about saying what you would actually say to the person. It is not a rehearsal. The idea is to give your feelings full reign to express themselves without the limitation

of having to be fair or rational or worrying what that person may do to you. Since you know that it is a fantasy, you can allow yourself to say and do anything. People often find themselves expressing intense feelings, even hatred and murderous rage. Yes, it is a fantasy, but if you do it sincerely you will find that it is also real. It can help to remove some of your emotional blocks, and it can make it easier to arrive at what you may actually want to say to the other person.

3. <u>Focusing:</u> This is a useful process for getting in touch with your inner experience when you can't identify a feeling. The idea is to look inside to find something called a felt sense. To get what a felt sense is, imagine that you get in your car and drive away from your home and have a vague feeling that you forgot something. It's not a feeling that you can name, yet it's there. That is a felt sense.

Here is an example of a situation in which you could use focusing. Let's say you and your partner Miriam are going out to dinner with two other couples. Miriam strongly suggests a particular restaurant and everyone goes along. During the evening you knew that you were uncomfortable, that something was bothering you, yet you didn't know what. Later that evening you decide to use the focusing process. You begin by trying to detect a vague, perhaps subtle, inner sense in the middle of your body. You put aside all effort to name feelings or think about what happened. You simply remain focused on the center point of the "body feeling" or "felt sense" and wait. You wait until there is a description that comes up in the form of a word or words or an image that captures the quality of the felt sense. You then check back with your body and see if the description is accurate. Then you wait for another description, coming from the same body point where you are focusing, that may be more "right on." You keep repeating this process until you learn something significant about your feelings.

In this example, let's imagine that you started with a sick feeling, and after going through several steps you got in touch with a sense of feeling controlled. This then led to an awareness that you were angry, which opened your awareness that you felt resentment toward Miriam for dominating. You also could have become clear that this was not just your reaction to that evening, but was a general feeling toward her. Theoretically, this could have led to insights about not only your relationship with Miriam, but your issues around domination and control as well. There is an excellent book called *Focusing* by Eugene Gendlin that gives a thorough description of the use of this technique.

4. <u>Taking responsibility for your feelings:</u>

A. Avoid claiming that your partner or someone else is the cause of your feelings.

While it is true that other people affect you and have a lot to do with your feelings, nobody can *make* you feel anything. Self-awareness means being willing to take responsibility for the part that you play in your reaction. Let's go back to the above hypothetical example of your relationship with your partner. Recognizing your resentment toward Miriam, feeling to some degree dominated by her, is important in itself. Expressing those feelings to Miriam would be a further valuable step. But even that doesn't go far enough. It does not give you the awareness that you need for yourself and the relationship. What you need is to own your role in the dance. How are you being passive, accommodating, or intimidated? How are you holding back your own assertiveness, etc.? There is strength in knowing that you are being honest in facing yourself and further strength in being willing to risk telling your partner about your insights. Also, even though you may begin by expressing resentment, sharing your part of the problem helps the relationship in two ways. First, it doesn't put the onus of blame on her, which often leads to a defensive reaction. Second, it enables her to understand you better, which gives her an opportunity to empathize with you. Instead of your being an innocent victim of domination and control, it becomes a mutual problem that you both work on.

B. Before reading further, make a list of statements beginning with the words "I can't" as they relate to anything in your life.

Now stop and make a list of statements beginning with the words "I have to." Notice how you feel in reaction to those lists.

Now go back and change the "I can't" statements to "I won't."

Now go back and change the "I have to" statements to "I choose to." Notice how you feel.

This is a further exercise in taking responsibility. The previous exercise had to do with taking responsibility for your feelings, whereas this exercise is taking responsibility for your choices. For example, if you changed "I can't get angry at my father" to "I won't get angry at my father" you might be more willing to look at the feelings involved in your choice. You may be afraid of his attack, worried that he will be very hurt, believe you would be an ungrateful son, etc.

Another example: If you changed "I have to spend Friday nights with my wife" to "I choose to…." you might be forced to look at all sorts of feelings, such as your dependency, fear of displeasing her, etc. Perhaps you are depriving yourself of something important to you, such as playing music or acting in a play in order to spend Friday nights with her. Facing the fact that you are making a choice enables you to look at your feelings and possibly change your behavior.

Statements such as "I can't" and "I have to" are often ways of playing helpless and taking the role of victim, which is a place in which you are stuck and nothing happens. Taking responsibility for your choices brings you closer to who you are, what you want, and what you feel. That opens you to the possibility of changing yourself, changing your relationship.

C. Speak for I.

When we discussed this approach earlier, I pointed out that merely making a judgmental statement about your partner's behavior is avoiding expressing your own feelings and wants, and that "speaking for I" is a way to prevent that mistake. Comments such as "You spend too much time talking on the telephone" or "you are drinking too much" say nothing about your feelings. You are leaving yourself out. If you speak for I, you might say, "When you talk on the phone all the time I feel rejected, like you don't want to be with me." Instead of saying, "You are drinking too much" you might say, "I see signs that you could be drifting back into alcoholism and it scares me." When you say what you are feeling in reaction to your partner you are putting yourself out there. You are taking responsibility for your feelings and showing yourself to her.

Another way that people put up a wall is to speak about feelings in generalizations, implying that anyone in the same situation would feel that way. Statements that begin with the words "you feel" or "you want" or "anybody would" are ways that you avoid taking responsibility for your own feelings, your own reactions. When you speak that way you are not present to yourself or to your partner. When you speak for yourself, saying "I feel" or "I want," your partner can empathize and connect with you.

Summary Guidelines

For the Man:

1. Pay attention to feelings such as hurt, fear, shame, and inadequacy. Having such feelings just means you are human. It does not mean you are weak or unmanly. Risk checking out your partner's attitude about this.

2. Remember that feelings have nothing to do with logic or rationality. Try to tell the difference between how you want to feel or think you should feel and how you actually feel.

3. If your partner says something to you that is disturbing or painful, see if you can allow yourself to experience the feeling while, at the same time, you listen to her.

4. Experiment with allowing yourself to stay in touch with painful feelings instead of immediately doing something to get rid of or lessen the pain. It can enable you to see yourself more clearly and more deeply.

5. Don't deny that your partner can hurt, threaten, and humiliate you. Actually, it's a sign that you are involved in the relationship.

6. If, in the heat of a dispute, your partner makes statements that seem to be condemning or rejecting you, check it out with her at the time or later. Find out if she meant it as a general conclusion about you or more as a feeling of the moment.

7. Notice if you are harboring disapproving or angry feelings toward your partner, and it is resulting in your being withdrawn from her. Remember that it is probably better for the

relationship to risk expressing those feelings because women are generally more hurt by distance than by open expression of negative feelings.

8. If, in the midst of an interaction, either you or your partner is overwhelmed with a flood of feelings, suggest that you take a break and come back to it later.

For the Woman:

1. Don't say things that imply that he is not "acting like a man." Remember that this threat could be a blow to his self-esteem and increase his defensiveness.

2. Let your man know that you consider it natural for him to have vulnerable feelings such as hurt, fear, and self-doubt and that they are not a sign of weakness or make him less of a man. When he risks being open with those feelings, show your appreciation and caring.

3. Try to avoid making absolute statements such as "you don't care about me" or "we just don't get along" in the heat of a dispute. Remember that men may take those statements as solid conclusions instead of something to be improved. He may feel condemned or despairing about the relationship.

4. Don't get caught in a rational argument about the facts. Put the emphasis on understanding each other's feelings and subjective reality.

5. When you discuss a family problem like finances or a problem with one of your kids, let your partner know that you are not expecting him to have an immediate solution. Make it clear

that you want to know that he is with you in sharing your concern.

6.   If your partner is being distant and you suspect he may be holding back negative feelings toward you, let him know that you are strong enough to handle his feelings and that you would rather that he come out with it than be distant.

8

Care for Your Relationship as a Separate Entity

I am constantly amazed by how often men hold back their feelings to avoid upsetting or getting a negative reaction from their partner, while being blind to or vastly underestimating the cost to the relationship by their holding back. Sometimes they are right that if they express what's on their mind there will be a temporary disruption in the relationship. But what they don't see is the insidious effect of not expressing themselves. They have yet to see the importance of treating their relationship as an entity that calls out for their attention and care. Until they do, building a strong connection with their partner will be difficult, if not impossible.

What happened between Charlie and Michelle as discussed in the first chapter is a good example of the cost of holding back. Charlie had been feeling hurt and resentful by Michelle's sexual rejection. Instead of telling Michelle what he felt, he tried to talk himself out of his feelings, which, of course, never works. The result was that he pulled back emotionally, and it came to a head when they went to a party. Despite his conscious effort to "behave himself," he ignored Michelle most of the time and was flirtatious with other women. His acting out behavior was a reaction to feelings that he was not willing to express openly. He had done this several times before. It was a familiar pattern. Deeply hurt, Michelle was in the process of pulling back from her investment in the marriage. In this case, the situation was finally salvaged by Charlie listening empathically to Michelle's feelings instead of just defending himself. The point is that their marriage had been in jeopardy because, for a long time, Charlie had not seen, or faced up to, the degree of damage to the relationship that resulted from not expressing his feelings directly to Michelle.

There are many reasons that men push back feelings in order to do what they believe will protect their partners, protect themselves, and/or protect their relationship. In the example of Roger and Jane, Roger was so afraid of expressing negative feelings toward Jane in a crushing way like his father had done that he pulled back from practically all family involvement. He was right in not wanting to be abusive, but what he blocked himself from seeing was that his solution of withdrawal, which was also an indirect expression of anger, almost destroyed his marriage. It was another example of the man trying to protect his partner, himself, and the marriage and not seeing that his protection was destroying the relationship. If he had faced the fact of how threatening his distancing behavior was to the marriage, he might have chosen to openly express his feelings of disapproval and resentment toward Jane, even if it meant that he had to risk being abusive like his father.

Here is the sad paradox: While Roger succeeded in not being overtly cutting like his father, under the surface he was manifesting a rejecting, belittling attitude toward Jane that *was* like his father. This is what often happens for us as men. We try to be different and not treat our partner the way we saw our parents treating us or treating each other, only to discover that we act the same way, though it may be indirect or subtle. Also, under Roger's superior attitude was an inner feeling of being over-powered and controlled by Jane. He lived out both roles: victim and victimizer, a common phenomenon.

Probably, Jane's reaction would have been like most women in a similar situation. She would rather that Roger had brought out into the open his angry and critical feelings, which, as is the case with most women, she sensed were there anyway. Even if his expression went beyond clean anger and was somewhat belittling or crushing, it would have been more tolerable and, ultimately, less painful than the rejection and unspoken contempt she had felt from him. Also, once he unleashed his negative feelings, his underlying feeling of being controlled by Jane would have been more accessible to him. Ideally, the thing to do in a similar situation would be to simply discuss the problem with your partner, explaining your fear of expressing negative feelings. While that is not always possible, whenever you can talk about your fear of expressing your negative feelings you are taking a major step toward treating your relationship as a separate and important entity.

- **Whatever your reason for holding back negative feelings toward your partner, if your relationship is at risk, come out with it. It beats damaging, and possibly losing, the relationship. Also, those feelings are probably coming out indirectly anyway.**

What the Woman Can Do:

If your partner is avoiding emotional contact with you, be suspicious that he is withholding some disapproval or anger. Check yourself to see if you are feeling afraid to have him openly express these feelings. Weigh that with how you are affected by his distance and the cost to the relationship. If you are ready to handle it, express your hunch that he is having some negative feeling toward you. Let him know that you are strong enough to take it and that you would rather have him express his feelings than be distant. If you don't feel able and willing to hear his negative feelings toward you, be aware that you could be contributing to his deciding that he has to push down what he really needs to say, which creates a wall between you. That would be something for you to work on in yourself and possibly discuss with your partner.

It is sad to see how often men deprive themselves of their need for emotional support in order to, as they see it, protect their partner from emotional distress. They accept their deprivation, not seeing that it is bad for their relationship. Ironically, it ends up hurting their partner more as well. Businessmen who are undergoing serious financial setbacks often keep it to themselves. They say things like, "Why make her anxious? It would serve no purpose." Sometimes the man is unhappy or having trouble at work and doesn't want to "burden her" with *his* problem. Here's an illustration.

Jerry came to me in a state of distress. He had gotten himself deeply in debt in his business, and Lori knew nothing about it. He was convinced that if he told her she would fall apart with anxiety. As disturbing and painful as it was to him to carry the full load of the problem by himself, he was convinced that telling Lori would make matters worse. So he made the mistake that many men make. He underestimated the cost to the relationship that resulted from his not sharing with his partner. When I spoke with Lori, I learned that she was feeling anxious because of her lack of knowledge about the actual financial situation of the business. She knew from past experience that Jerry would not tell her if there were a business failure. Also, she felt shut out by him. He was withdrawn, and she could sense that he was worried, but she could not penetrate the wall between them. The distance and loneliness they both felt was a threat to their marriage.

As we explored the situation together, Jerry finally faced the fact that his solution of silence was causing an intolerable risk to the relationship, and that he had to risk being open with Lori. When he finally told her the truth about their financial situation, including the debt, she was anxious. But she did not "fall apart" as he had imagined. She went through a period of both anxiety and anger about having been kept in the dark. Yet they were able to talk about the situation in a more open and honest way than they had ever done before, which brought them closer. From that place of increased trust and closeness, they were able to share some of the feelings behind their behavior.

Jerry was able to see that he had been not only protecting Lori but also protecting *himself* from her negative judgment of him. Behind that was his own pride and perfectionism, much of which was based on a common distorted view of what constitutes being a man: "A man should be able to deal with his worries and anxieties by himself and shouldn't need to lean on anybody." Like many men, Jerry paid a large price for this misguided view of masculinity. And it could have ended up wrecking his marriage. The truth is that everyone needs support, and men certainly need support from their wives.

- **It can be feeding your ego to think of yourself as a self-sufficient man who handles the finances and protects his family. But if it means carrying the full burden of responsibility, you are depriving yourself of the support that you need, while probably harming your relationship.**

It often happens that when a man risks disclosing hidden feelings, his partner also feels safe in disclosing her unexpressed feelings. That is what happened with Lori. After Jerry told her the truth, she felt willing and able to look at how she had been contributing to the problem. She was able to admit that there was a side of her that did not want to know about Jerry's business problems. She could see that she indirectly gave Jerry the message that she could not handle the anxiety. She also became clear that Jerry's "protection" was not really in her best interest, since it helped to keep her partly in the role of a child rather than an adult. When she married Jerry she was looking for a man who would provide the guidance and protection that she didn't get from her father. She recognized that by staying in that dependent role she missed out on the satisfaction of knowing that she was needed and could provide comfort and nurturance to Jerry when he was scared and worried. Jerry's so-called protection was actually harmful to her by blocking her emotional development. The more she got involved in facing the realities of their financial situation, and the more she experienced herself as nurturing and supporting Jerry, the stronger she felt.

Also, Jerry gradually felt less and less attachment to the burden and the pedestal as "the great provider and protector." By taking the risk of causing Lori great distress, he ended up doing her a big favor. They became more relaxed with each other, more equal and much closer. What was the key that broke the logjam? It was the fact that Jerry finally realized that his relationship was in jeopardy, and that it was related to keeping his business anxieties walled off from Lori. He knew that he had to do something different, that he had to risk telling the truth to Lori for the sake of their relationship. This story has a happy ending, but it doesn't always work that way. Often men never recognize that keeping their business or work insecurities to themselves instead of sharing it with their partners is putting up a wall that can destroy their relationship.

What the Woman Can Do:

When your partner seems distressed or is not talking about his business or work, consider that he might be deliberately keeping something from you. Does he share his fears and uncertainties about his business with you? Ask yourself if he may be protecting you. Also ask yourself if in some way you may be colluding in an unspoken system or rule that says he is not supposed to burden you with concerns about his business. Are you giving the impression that you don't want the anxiety that goes with knowing that things in his work are not going well? Consider that this "protection" could be keeping a wall between you and could be blocking your emotional development.

Earlier in the book I talked about a tragic situation in which Dennis and Betty lost their eight-year-old daughter in an automobile accident. Dennis did everything he could to minister to Betty and take care of her feelings. He consistently held on to the role of protector or caretaker, never allowing himself to feel and express *his* pain so that he could also lean on Betty for comfort and support. It never became a shared, mutual process. Not only was he deprived, but his actions also weren't meeting his partner's deep need for connection with him during this painful time, and their relationship suffered. It was a situation that could have brought them closer together, if only Dennis had been thinking about the need to care not just for Betty but for their relationship as an entity. Instead, they grew further and further apart and finally divorced. Another tragic loss!

- **When both of you are experiencing emotional pain, don't keep your feelings to yourself in order to take care of your partner. In most cases you will be creating a wall that deprives you both of what you really need, which is to connect and touch each other by sharing your feelings.**

The Power of Emotional Teamwork

Generally, women tend to be more oriented to relationships than men, so it may be easier for them to grasp the concept of nourishing the relationship as a separate entity. Women, then, can naturally reach out and help men learn how to focus on what is best for the relationship. The greatest benefit, however, comes when both partners identify with the relationship as an *equal entity*. You know that you are together in the understanding that your relationship stands on three legs: "what is good for you," "what is good for me," and "what is good for the relationship." Judith Wallenstein, Ph.D., who has extensively studied the American family, pinpointed that ingredient in her research. She interviewed fifty couples who had built "long-lasting, happy marriages." She found that in a good marriage each partner must learn to identify with the other and both together to identify with the marriage. The couples she studied seemed to carry an image of the "marriage as a separate presence that required continued attention and nurture, like a healthy garden."

When both partners are together in attending to the relationship as a separate entity, many problems related to guilt or fear of selfishness disappear. Let's say that you feel that your needs are not being met or that she is doing something you don't like and would like her to change. You both know that if you hold back your feelings it will probably lead to a toxic, negative reaction like your becoming emotionally walled off and/or finding that your disapproval or anger comes out indirectly. Then expressing your feelings becomes something that you both know that you need to do for the good of the relationship. It is part of the tacit agreement or understanding that you have with each other. That relieves you from the deadly trap of feeling that expressing your feelings amounts to meeting your own needs at her expense. You know that she trusts you to not just be looking out for yourself, but to be also considering what is best for the relationship. Knowing that she trusts you in that way makes it a lot easier to express feelings that may be painful or threatening to her. Also, your openness could lead to a change in her behavior, which would benefit the relationship. Caring about the relationship as an equal entity is really another way of caring about each other.

- **When you both know that you are looking out for the relationship as well as yourself, it is easier and safer to say things**

that may be painful or hard for your partner to hear. Ultimately, it's what is best for both of you.

Intimate relationships, after the initial romantic attraction, are by their very nature emotionally challenging and fraught with difficulty. We are all conditioned beings, and our deepest personality traits are formed from early experiences, especially from our family relationships. When, as an adult, we get involved in an intimate or committed relationship, all the old images, feelings, and defensive reactions get reenacted. If your partner gets annoyed you may experience it as a painful attack. Moderate criticism could cause you to feel unworthy or ashamed. Simple requests could seem like efforts to dominate or control. Normal separations could bring up fears of abandonment. When your partner asks you to be more open you may feel in danger of being manipulated or smothered.

The idea that we can and should grow out of, and be free of, all of those sensitive reactions is an illusion. It is a destructive tyranny that we impose on ourselves and our partners. Of course it is possible to change, and we do overcome some early feelings and defensive reactions through life experience. Close relationships can be the best way to modify and sometimes correct unhealthy influences from the past. But the truth is that some of those early sensitive areas and patterns are deeply imbedded and will never be completely gone, no matter how hard we try. We need to accept that as just being human.

Couples who lack that understanding get in a lot of difficulty with each other. Let's say that, like the example from earlier in the book with Laura and Frank, your partner gets upset when you go away on business trips. She puts pressure on you to take fewer trips or to bring her along with you. You react by feeling smothered and controlled. You both could be stuck in the feeling that things can never be all right between you unless the other one changes. You tell yourself that she needs to get over her clinging, dependent behavior.

She thinks that you need to change your feelings toward her so that you want to be with her more. Nothing changes. Both of you feel not understood and not cared for. It has a toxic effect on your relationship.

Couples who know and accept each other's emotional baggage do a much better job at handling comparable situations. Instead of focusing on who shouldn't feel the way they feel and who needs to change, they have a totally different orientation. Their attitude is that their partner has a right to her feelings no matter what, and you have a right to your feelings. You may think that she is misperceiving the situation and over-reacting. It doesn't matter—you are not judgmental or dismissive of her feelings. Both partners recognize that their feelings may be, at least in part, the result of sensitive reactions from early background experiences. It's not that you like the way your partner is. It may bother you a lot. You wish she were different. At the same time, you accept the fact that we all have to deal with stirred up reactions stemming from our backgrounds. That's a vital part of regarding your relationship as a separate entity.

In the previous example, the man could be aware that his partner's sensitivity about being left is tied to her experience of being abandoned as a child. She could be aware that he could be over-reacting to her pressure on him to take fewer trips because of his early experience of a mother who was very dependent and kept him tied to her. Behind that, there can be the recognition that, at the deepest level, we are all struggling, vulnerable human beings trying to survive the best we can. That awareness, that non-judgmental acceptance of each other's emotional baggage, makes it a lot easier to be empathic. And, as I have been often saying, when there is an empathic connection everything changes. This couple would feel more positive toward each other, and they would be in a much better position to work out changes in behavior if that were needed.

• **All of us carry sensitive feelings and reactions from our early background that will never completely change. If you and your partner understand that, you will do a much better job of being empathic and working out your differences.**

The example of Robert and Linda was a good illustration of wholesome handling of strong feelings. Robert got very angry with Linda for talking to him in a way that he experienced as belittling and bossy. Linda knew that this was a very touchy area for Robert since he had grown up with an intimidating and critical father. When Robert got angry, instead of just being caught up in her own feelings she had the foresight of recognizing that she had pushed Robert's sensitive button. She was able to put her own feelings and judgments aside and be empathic. She listened and responded by saying that it was not okay for her to talk down to him.

After pausing long enough to make sure that Robert was finished and available to listen to her, Linda brought up her feelings. She told Robert how she resented his tendency to tune out in situations that were important to her, such as that upcoming supervisors' meeting. She felt that *she* was being belittled by *him*. Robert was also able to listen and to understand her sensitive reaction in two ways. First, he knew himself well enough to realize that, like his father, he had a tendency to not give much attention to things that mattered to his partner. He saw that it was a put-down, and he had a vague recognition that he was in some way treating Linda like his father treated him. As in the previous example with Roger and Jane, he was very sensitive to feeling belittled, like what he experienced from his father, yet found himself doing it indirectly to her. He also knew that Linda was very sensitive about not being taken seriously, since she grew up in a family in which her parents had only a superficial understanding and appreciation of who she was. As it turned out, what could have been a painful disruption ended in a warm empathic connection.

The two things that were crucial in enabling that to happen were, first, that they knew and were respectful of their own and each other's sensitivities. Second, they trusted each other in knowing that if one of them expressed their feelings it was done with some consideration for what was best *for the relationship*. They had that mutual foundation of security.

- **No matter how hard we try to not treat our partners in negative ways like the way we felt treated by our parents, we will probably end up doing it at times, though it may be indirectly.**

Basing the relationship on what is good for me, what is good for you, and what is good for the relationship also can take some of the pressure off concerns about whether you are being irrational or unfair. That came up in the example of something that happened with me and my wife Carol. I was bothered by the fact that I had been doing all the dishes for some time while Carol was spending more time with her creative writing. I didn't feel comfortable complaining since Carol was the one who usually did the bulk of the household chores and was supportive of *my* writing. I had the feeling that if I said anything about it I would be inconsiderate, unfair, and even childish. I knew that I was harboring resentment, and I noticed that, in holding back my feelings, I was beginning to become emotionally distant, which, I was well aware, was bad for us as a couple. I realized that, despite any feelings of being unfair or looking foolish, I had to speak up.

Fortunately, I had the safety of knowing that Carol trusted me to not say anything without some consideration of what was best for the relationship. Also, I knew myself well enough to be aware that I was very sensitive about being dominated or controlled. Both of those factors made it easier to risk expressing my feelings. Neither of us was stuck in the requirement to be rational and fair, and we were able to work it out in a way that was considerate of each other's feelings.

- **To work together as a team, and to be fully yourself, means that sometimes it is necessary to risk expressing feelings that are irrational, unfair, or may make you look foolish.**

Another example of a couple avoiding a painful disruption by recognizing and accepting their partner's sensitive issues occurred with Michelle and Charlie. They decided to spend an evening at home watching a romantic movie with the expectation that after the movie they would make love. When the movie was over Michelle complained that he had not touched her the entire time that they were watching the show, even though she had made several overtures. Charlie got very upset. He experienced her complaint as a critical, angry attack. He felt as if she was accusing him of being cold and rejecting and had ruined any chance of lovemaking. At first, he was very defensive, arguing that he *had* touched her during the show. Michelle realized that he was over-reacting and she said that to him. She then asked him what he was feeling. He said that he felt criticized and condemned.

The combination of Michelle's calmness and her telling him that he was over-reacting enabled Charlie to also calm down and consider that he could be over-reacting. They both were conscious of his background of being devastated by a father who would often become suddenly angry and dismissive. He was able to listen and receive Michelle's explanation that she had felt only mildly annoyed and hurt that he had not been touching her, and that she had not considered that their evening was ruined. Charlie also knew that Michelle's insecurity stemmed from her background. He knew that she had a tendency to doubt that she is loved and sexually desired. That enabled him to see that her behavior could have been partly the result of *her* sensitivity.

Early in their relationship, incidents like this would have resulted in a painful disruption. Now, they were able to make constructive use of knowing and accepting each other's sensitive wounds, and they were able to come together in a loving way.

Unfortunately, it is also possible to use knowledge of your partner's background in a destructive way. Attributing your partner's reactions to early conditioning can be a way of making your partner wrong. "You are over-sensitive and distorting. I wasn't being critical." "You are being demanding like your mother." "It's just your old fear of rejection." Statements like these can be a way of denying that your partner may also be reacting accurately to what you are doing. In that way you avoid looking at how you are part of the "dance."

What was wholesome in Charlie and Michelle's example was that they were not focused on proving that they were right and their partner wrong. They had the teamwork orientation. They both knew that their emotional baggage could have been operating, and they didn't concern themselves with having to decide *whose* sensitivity was kicking in more, or who was the one who was doing the most misinterpreting and over-reacting. It was enough that they recognized that they both were part of the problem.

- **When your partner seems to be over-reacting to your behavior, don't assume that it is just her emotional baggage and sensitivity and that she is not also accurate about you. It could be a way of defending yourself by making you right and her wrong.**

Summary Guidelines

For the Man:

1. Look upon your relationship as standing on three legs: what is good for you, what is good for your partner, what is good for the relationship. It is treating the relationship as a separate entity that needs to be nourished.

2. Be aware that we all carry emotional baggage, mostly from early family relationships, that come to the surface and reoccur when we become intimately involved with someone.

3. While you may be able to resolve some emotional issues from the past, give up the tyranny of thinking that you or your partner should be able to overcome all of that.

4. Recognize that it is natural, with the exception of early romantic illusion, that there will be some things about your partner that you don't like.

5. Be careful to avoid using knowledge of your partner's past in a negative way, to "prove" that her behavior is invalid or wrong. That is self-defensive and can be destructive.

6. Men need emotional support. Don't deprive yourself of that support by keeping your concerns about work and finances to yourself.

7. Trying to protect your partner from distress by keeping your work or financial worries to yourself could be "protecting" her from emotional maturity. That would not be in her best interest or in the best interest of the relationship.

8. When something traumatic happens to both of you, it is important that you share your feelings with each other. Not coming together in that way could cause a serious rift in your relationship.

9. Your partner's recognition that you care for the relationship helps to free you from the trap of guilt that comes from the feeling that you are expressing yourself at her expense.

10. Mutual caring for the relationship as a separate entity also makes it easier to risk being unfair or irrational.

For the Woman:

1. Because it may be easier for you to grasp the concept of nourishing the relationship as a separate entity, you can help him understand this perspective.

2. Let your partner know that you would rather that he express negative feelings toward you than be emotionally distant. Check yourself to see if you may be giving him the impression that you can't handle those feelings.

3. Let your partner know that you want him to share his concerns about his work.

4. Make it clear to him that you want to be an equal partner in knowing the reality of your financial situation so that he is not carrying the emotional burden alone. Check yourself to see if you are giving him the impression that you want to be "taken care of" rather than share that stress.

9

Open to the Spiritual Dimension of Your Relationship

Throughout this book, we have been looking at why empathy is so important in our relationships and how practicing it more consistently can build a deeper intimate connection with our partner. Now I want to focus on why empathy is so vitally important in our individual lives. Just why is empathy such a basic and compelling human need?

At the deepest level, being responded to empathically is being seen and being known as you are. It is a critical and fundamental human need, a need that goes back to infancy. Infants come into the world helplessly tied to and dependent upon their mothers. They rely on their mothers to respond accurately to their feelings and needs. Mothers do this by staying attuned to a range of non-verbal signals, some quite subtle. This process is the most basic form of empathy. The more accurately attuned the mother is, the more secure the infant feels, and, even this early, begins to develop a healthy sense of self. As the well known psychoanalyst D.N. Winnicott described it, the capacity to experience *a sense of one's own being as real* depends on the mother doing so first, mirroring back to the child who he is and what he is like. Thus, the mother's empathy, in this most basic form, is crucial in the infant's healthy development.

Human beings, especially infants and children, need a clear sense of being known and connected in order to survive. Children whose parents are continually lacking in empathy often become deeply disturbed. They are likely to have a weak sense of self, and they tend to doubt the validity of their feelings. They may feel painfully different and alienated from others. This basic need, to be seen and known for who we are, is present throughout our lives, and we especially need that from our intimate partners.

The Right to Be

In the process of growing up, we erect walls that protect us from the kind of painful disruptions that we experienced when our parents were unempathic. Realistically, all parents fail to be empathic at times. While as adults we are not as dependent and helpless as we were as children, that vulnerability is still there to some degree, and it gets stirred up in intimate relationships. Early family issues that you thought were buried or resolved come up again with your mate. The experience of being misunderstood and not accepted by your partner can reactivate old feelings of self-doubt. If you are someone who has been deeply wounded in your childhood, that self-doubt can reach the level of doubting your reality, and even your sanity.

- **Empathy is a basic human need. Your partner's failure to be empathic could be threatening not only because of your need for connection, but also because it could undermine trust in your own reality.**

There may be times when you are having feelings that you are critical or ashamed of. You could doubt that whatever it is that you are experiencing has a right to exist. Those are the times that your partner's empathy may be especially important. It could mean not only that you are connected with her, but that you have her support and the strength that comes with it in knowing that *your feelings are legitimate.* That reinforces your sense of yourself as a valid, worthwhile human being. You may not like some of the feelings that get stirred up in you and your partner may not like the fact that you have those feelings. You may want to work on understanding and changing some of those feelings. While that doesn't mean that you have the right to behave any way that you want, it does mean that you have the right to feel what you feel.

- **You always have the right to your feelings, no matter what those feelings are based on, or whether you like or approve of those feelings. Partners need to support that right in each other.**

In basic empathy, you put your own feelings aside in order to listen and understand how she feels and sees things. You may be doing this out of genuine compassion or, at times, your listening may just be good strategy. In either case, you could be having your own reactions and judgments. You may disapprove of your partner's behavior. You may be thinking about how it affects you. You may be wishing she didn't feel or act the way she does, for your sake or for hers. You may even be thinking of your own shortcomings or what can be done to correct the situation. In order to empathize, you put these reactions sufficiently aside so that you can see things from her perspective. This in itself is valuable. If most people practiced this basic form of empathy, relationships would be much improved.

As I've said before, it is possible to empathize with your partner at a deeper level so that you are fully attending to experiencing her as she is. When you do that, there is no judgment and no agenda. Even the wish that she were different is completely in the background or not there at all. Your only goal is to listen, to see, to know her. It would be like listening to music with total absorption. The speaker can experience the listener's full, uncontaminated attention as if he is saying to her, "You have the right to be who you are." It can be experienced as "I know you and I choose to be in relationship with you." That experience is the fertile ground of intimacy and love.

- **In deeper empathy you are totally absorbed in listening, with no judgment or wish that your partner be different. Your only goal is to see and know her.**

Spirituality: Connecting Deeper

In practicing the kind of deeper intimacy I have been describing, you are moving to the spiritual dimension. When you experience your partner from the spiritual dimension, you are in contact with her inner core or essence, beyond all personality attributes. From that place, awareness of differences—things you like and don't like about her—don't matter. At those times you are totally present. There is no question of your right to be who you are or her right to be who she is. It is just a given. You experience a connection that is beyond your separate personalities. It is a meeting of two equal beings. This can be called I-Thou relating, described by Martin Buber in his seminal book *I and Thou*.

In those moments of relating we are free of our ordinary view of separateness and in touch with an expanded sense of oneness. It is a state of spiritual consciousness beyond mental concepts and images, usually arrived at through practices of meditation and/or prayer. Periods of profound presence and connection with our partners sometimes occur spontaneously. It can happen during life-threatening or tragic events, moments of crisis, the birth of a child, or even at the beginning stages of falling in love. It may or may not involve an organized religion or having particular religious beliefs.

- **Through spiritual awareness, it is possible to connect with your partner beyond the level of the personality to a deeper sense of equality and oneness.**

Pursuing a spiritual path can not only bring about periods of heightened connection with your partner, it can also lead to an enduring change in consciousness. That change can give valuable support to the relationship. When you and your partner experience a connection beyond the level of personality attributes, you have a sense of deep meaning and trust in the rightness of your being together. And, if both of you are committed to spiritual growth, that level of connection can help make your relationship part of your highest purpose.

Viewing yourself and the relationship from a larger context of spiritual meaning and purpose also has definite advantages in dealing with the inevitable conflicts of everyday life together. The problems are still there, but they lose their all-encompassing importance. Negative comments about you may still hurt, but you are less likely to experience them as complete rejection or evidence that you are a total loser. The threat is defused by the fact that you no longer judge yourself so harshly since you are aware that who you are is more than your conditioning, your personality characteristics. And if you know that your partner also has that perspective, you feel further supported in your self-acceptance. What often happens is that the old wounds still get triggered but are less painful, and you recover faster.

- **When you know that you are more than your personality, you are more accepting of yourself, and your partner's negative comments about you don't hurt as much, or not at all.**

Couples who hold the consciousness of themselves and each other as more than their personality traits can feel safer in exposing their fears, their sense of inadequacy, or whatever their particular foibles may be. This safety and openness enables them to be much closer, while at the same time it furthers their spiritual growth. There is a natural humility that comes from openly acknowledging our human vulnerability and perhaps allowing our heart to break open. When we do that, we manifest our deeper selves and become more loving.

Sometimes, we may experience a shift in the way we love our partners so that we have a sense of *love itself* rather than who is loving whom. Then, there is no question of whether your partner is "the right person." What matters is that you are able to enter the realm of love. Questions like "Am I happily married?" or even "Am I happy?" can lose their gripping importance. Those concerns may be replaced by a different orientation, which focuses on the issue of "Am I fulfilling my higher purpose?" That kind of perspective can take a lot of pressure off your relationship as *the* source of your life fulfillment. Asking your relationship to be the "be all and end all" can only cause frustration and sorrow anyway. There needs to be other important ways that you find meaning and self-expression in your life. That includes the basic human need for the expanded perspective of spiritual consciousness.

• **The spiritual orientation can take pressure off your relationship by orienting you to a higher purpose in the fulfillment of your life.**

As we consider such wonderful possibilities, it is important to keep in mind that anything, no matter how valuable and legitimate, can also be used defensively. That certainly includes spirituality. While a goal of spiritual practice is to see beyond the level of personality, it is important to recognize real feelings. To deny, to bury, or try to rise above those feelings in the name of spirituality is another avoidance. It can be a difficult trap because you may be able to temporarily feel better by telling yourself that you are beyond certain feelings and in touch with a greater truth. And if you are not able to escape the feelings that you don't like, you could tell yourself that you are not spiritual enough. Another possible pitfall is that your effort to see beyond the personality could be depriving yourself of the juiciness and satisfactions of personal friendships and personal love. Those are some of the reasons that, if you are on a spiritual path, it is important to monitor yourself with the aid of a spiritual guide, a spiritual peer group, or a therapist.

- **Spiritual practice can be used defensively as a way of escaping from your feelings. Make sure you have some external source of guidance to check on that.**

One of the areas where your personality issues and conflicts with your partner can become the most highly charged is in sex. If spiritual consciousness is helping to lessen your self-critical judgments and judgments of your partner, obviously that will also help your sex life. In our culture, we tend to emphasize sex as a bodily need and source of pleasure, sometimes requiring certain skills, and, hopefully, accompanied by feelings of love. We use the expression "making love," but what does that mean? Spiritual consciousness can make a real difference there. From that orientation, you and your partner deciding to "make love" can mean, "Let's enter the creation and experience of love." Coming together sexually can then be an integration of physical pleasure, personal feelings of love, and something beyond, to love itself. It can free you from conflicts and self-doubts that come from splitting bodily desires from something more in the realm of love and "the sacred." It can be experienced as a connection with your partner that is personal while also going beyond the personal to a sense of spiritual union.

Let's consider another way that the spiritual orientation can help you build a stronger connection with your partner. It can not only help you and your partner by making your everyday conflicts less gripping and disturbing, but, beyond that, it can provide a valuable grounding and support, which make it easier to face and overcome old wounds and defensive patterns. It can be part of the goal to help ourselves and our partners realize our true nature beyond our conditioned personality.

Connecting with your partner in a way that surpasses personal attributes and dissolves separateness can be a powerful, freeing, and illuminating experience. Your connection can encompass the personal, yet extend beyond the personal to greater reality.

Summary Guidelines

1. Empathy is a crucial and fundamental human need that goes back to infancy.

2. Children whose parents continually lack empathy become deeply disturbed. They have a weak sense of self and doubt the validity of their feelings.

3. Your partner's failure to empathize with you could activate your old wounds and self-doubts and make you question the validity of your feelings and even your reality.

4. Your partner especially needs your support when she is self-critical or ashamed of her feelings. You and your partner have a right to your feelings no matter what those feelings are or where they come from.

5. In deeper levels of empathy you listen with total absorption, uncontaminated by any agenda other than to see and know her.

6. It is possible to connect with your partner at a level of consciousness beyond personality attributes. It is a spiritual meeting of two equal beings, sometimes referred to as "I-Thou."

7. Spiritual consciousness enables you to be more self-accepting, which makes you less prone to be threatened by disapproval or conflicts with your partner.

8. Couples with a spiritual orientation can feel their relationship supported by the realization that they are sharing in the goal of fulfilling a higher purpose.

9. There is a risk of spirituality being used defensively to escape from feelings that you don't like. It is important that you have an outside source of guidance to guard against that.

10. A spiritual orientation can improve your sexual love-making by diminishing the pull of personality conflicts and by helping you to integrate the physical with the sacred.

Epilogue

Not surprisingly, the time I have spent writing this book, supposedly to teach others, has been a valuable learning experience for me both as a therapist and in my personal life. Some of the times when I thought I was being empathic with a client I later learned that my empathy was limited or compromised by other hidden agendas. My own needs or defenses were operating under the surface, and even my desire to be helpful or supportive was an impediment for some people. When I recognized that and was able to put aside all other agendas to simply be empathic, the outcome was very powerful.

An exchange I had with Carolyn, a young professional woman, provides a good illustration. She could see nothing positive in her life and saw no reason to live. I listened, trying to empathize with her despair, and then I would also point out something positive in her life, such as an accomplishment at work or a recent caring response she had received from a friend. This went on for two months, with no sign of change. I was very concerned about her, and considered the danger of suicide.

One day I took a risk. I chose to just empathize without trying to be supportive or encouraging in any way. When she made statements about how useless her life was, I would say things like "how awful" or "what a terrible feeling" or "I see what you mean." I didn't add anything hopeful or positive. As our session ended, she looked as if she had come out of a dark hole. She shot up from her chair, stepped closer to me, looked me directly in the eye and said, "*Finally,* I feel understood!" From that day on, Carolyn made real progress in her therapy.

Leland, a bright, competent young man, described how he was a complete failure in all aspects of his life. I resisted the temptation to point out ways in which he had been doing well, both in his work and in his social life. Instead, I just listened empathically. It struck a responsive chord. "I really appreciate that you didn't do what everybody else in my life does," Leland said. "They're always trying to tell me all the *good* things." From that moment on, Leland trusted me more and our relationship was on a deeper basis.

Another example occurred with Richard, a client who would often disregard his own judgment and follow the lead of others. I frequently commented on this pattern, with very limited change in his behavior. Finally, I did something different. I pointed out that his feeling that he couldn't trust his own reality and had to follow the direction of others must be "very painful." Previously, my empathy had been limited. Now, I was with him on the level of his *feelings*, which has the quality of compassion. It made all the difference. It opened the door to his feeling much safer and open with me, and was the beginning of real progress in his therapy. The power of empathy again had made a dramatic impact.

Empathy continues to have a profound influence in my personal life as well. Naturally, I find it a lot easier to teach other people than to follow the teachings myself. Am I always able to be empathic with my partner? No. And as much as *you* try to follow the teachings in this book, you probably won't always be consistent with it either. The point, for all of us, is to keep in mind the positive impact empathy can have and to use it wherever and whenever we can. I hope that our discussions throughout this book will continue to be useful to you along the way. As my partner says when I start acting defensive instead of being empathic, "Read your book!"

Contact the Author

You may contact Dr. Maslow at:
A.R. Bob Maslow, Ph.D.
914 East High St.
Charlottesville, VA 22902
434-979-0276

978-0-595-41492-5
0-595-41492-3

Printed in the United States
63791LVS00001B/1-99